Practical System Programming with C

Pragmatic Example Applications in Linux and Unix-Based Operating Systems

Sri Manikanta Palakollu

Apress®

Practical System Programming with C: Pragmatic Example Applications in Linux and Unix-Based Operating Systems

Sri Manikanta Palakollu
freelance, Hanuman Junction, Hanuman Junction, 521105, Andhra Pradesh, India

ISBN-13 (pbk): 978-1-4842-6320-4   ISBN-13 (electronic): 978-1-4842-6321-1
https://doi.org/10.1007/978-1-4842-6321-1

Managing Director, Apress Media LLC: Welmoed Spahr
Acquisitions Editor: Steve Anglin
Development Editor: Matthew Moodie
Coordinating Editor: Mark Powers

Cover designed by eStudioCalamar

Cover image by Ricardo Gomez on Unsplash (www.unsplash.com)

Distributed to the book trade worldwide by Apress Media, LLC, 1 New York Plaza, New York, NY 10004, U.S.A. Phone 1-800-SPRINGER, fax (201) 348-4505, e-mail orders-ny@springer-sbm.com, or visit www.springeronline.com. Apress Media, LLC is a California LLC and the sole member (owner) is Springer Science + Business Media Finance Inc (SSBM Finance Inc). SSBM Finance Inc is a **Delaware** corporation.

For information on translations, please e-mail booktranslations@springernature.com; for reprint, paperback, or audio rights, please e-mail bookpermissions@springernature.com.

Apress titles may be purchased in bulk for academic, corporate, or promotional use. eBook versions and licenses are also available for most titles. For more information, reference our Print and eBook Bulk Sales web page at http://www.apress.com/bulk-sales.

Any source code or other supplementary material referenced by the author in this book is available to readers on GitHub via the book's product page, located at www.apress.com/9781484263204. For more detailed information, please visit http://www.apress.com/source-code.

Printed on acid-free paper

Table of Contents

About the Author

Sri Manikanta Palakollu is a programmer and software developer with experience in C, C++, Java, and Python as well as Linux and POSIX-based systems-level programming. He is a tech reviewer for various tech book publishers. He has written many technical articles on data science, programming, and cybersecurity. Sri Manikanta has won a national-level hackathon and contributes to various open source projects.

Acknowledgments

I would like to thank my savior, the **Lord Jesus Christ**, for giving me the strength, knowledge, wisdom, and ability to write this book. I would like to express my deepest gratitude to the Apress team: Steve Anglin (Acquisition Editor), Mark Powers (Coordinating Editor), and Matthew Moodie (Development Editor) for giving me this opportunity and providing constant support during the entire development process. Thanks to my technical reviewer for his efforts in reviewing this book.

Special thanks to my friends *Sai Vardhan Poloju*, *Aravind Medamoni*, *Vamsi Thanjagari*, and *PTS Vaishnavi* for helping me during this journey.

Thanks to my spiritual parents, *Rev. Amos Varma* and *Amrutha*, for their constant prayer support and love. I would like to thank my parents, *Basaveswara Rao* and *Vijaya Lakshmi*, for their love and support. I thank my brother *Santhosh* and my sister *Sri Lakshmi* for helping me design the diagrams in this book.

—Sri Manikanta Palakollu

Introduction

The main goal of this book is to introduce system programming using the C language. The topics covered in this book teach you how to programmatically manipulate Linux and POSIX-based operating systems. The wide variety of topics include

- The basics of the Linux operating system

- Multithreaded programming in C

- Deadlocks

- An introduction to POSIX standards

- The need for processes and signals

- Various IPC techniques

- Developing client-server architecture using TCP and UDP protocols

The prerequisites for learning the concepts discussed in this book are

- A basic knowledge of the C programming language

- A basic knowledge of operating systems

CHAPTER 1

Introduction to the Linux Environment

Linux is an open source, Unix-like operating system based on the Linux kernel. It was developed by Linus Torvalds in 1991. It is used in personal computers, mainframe computers, supercomputers, Android mobile devices, routers, and embedded systems. Linux is a very lightweight and powerful kernel that effectively communicates with software programs through any kind of hardware.

The growth of Linux is increasing with the relative growth of technology. IoT devices like Raspberry PI use the Linux kernel with a variety of Linux distributions. Since Linux is open source, you can modify the source code as you require. There are more than 500 active Linux distributions (a.k.a. distros) available on the market; most of them are free. Some distributions require payment for advanced features. The best examples of Linux kernel-based distros are Ubuntu, Linux Mint, Fedora, Debian, and Arch Linux.

This chapter discusses the following topics.

- The Linux architecture
- Kernel types
- Linux kernel vs. other OS kernels
- File handling utilities
- Process utilities
- Backup utilities

© Sri Manikanta Palakollu 2021
S. M. Palakollu, *Practical System Programming with C*, https://doi.org/10.1007/978-1-4842-6321-1_1

Getting Familiar with the Linux Architecture

The Linux architecture consists of four layers (see Figure 1-1).

- Hardware layer
- Kernel
- Shell
- System library

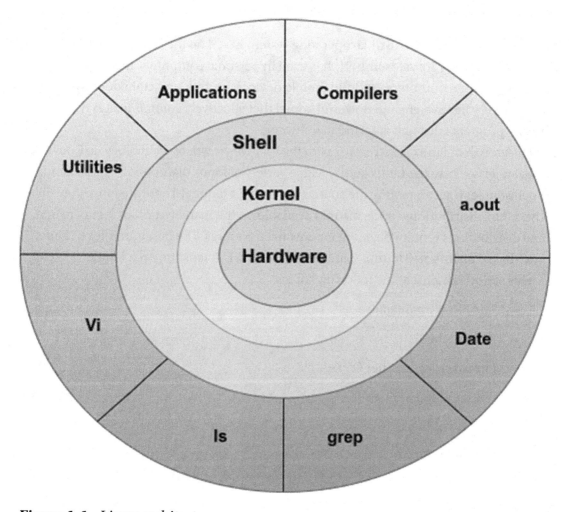

Figure 1-1. *Linux architecture*

Hardware Layer

This layer consists of drivers that are required to handle peripheral devices like the mouse, keyboards, hard disks, SSD, printers, and so forth.

Kernel

The kernel is the heart of the operating system; without kernels, you are not able to communicate with application programs and the operating system on hardware devices. The kernel acts as an interface between hardware components and application programs. A kernel has the following functionalities.

- I/O management

- Process management

- Resource management

- Device management

I/O Management

A kernel has several I/O management advantages that make a system more intelligent.

- It provides I/O scheduling with standard scheduling algorithms.

- It effectively buffers the data transfer between two devices.

- It caches data, which improves the performance of the system.

- It handles errors and issues when a user performs an illegal operation.

Process Management

On an operating system, process management is important in performing a certain task or activity requested by the user; for example, executing a program, playing music, or editing a video or photo using a software application. These activities are represented by tasks that need to be executed by the CPU with the help of the processor. The kernel properly manages the threads without any conflicts.

Resource Management

When a task is performed in an operating system, it requires system resources. The CPU allocates the required resources to perform the task. The kernel optimizes the resources during process synchronization.

Device Management

A peripheral device requires a specific driver to connect to the operating system. The kernel maintains the device drivers so that they properly connect when needed.

Types of Kernels

There are five types of kernels. Each type has advantages and disadvantages.

- Monolithic kernel

- Microkernel

- Hybrid kernel

- Nanokernel

- Exokernel

Monolithic Kernels

In a *monolithic kernel*, the memory space between the user and the kernel services is not shared. The advantage of this kernel is that memory management, CPU scheduling, and file management is done through system calls only. A monolithic kernel works faster because it acts under a single memory space. The disadvantage is that creating new services is a difficult task.

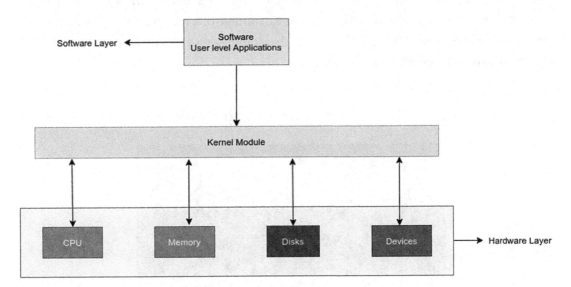

Figure 1-2. *Monolithic kernel architecture*

Microkernels

Before discussing microkernels, let's talk about kernel space and user space.

Kernel Space

The space that is allocated to run the core part of an operating system is called
kernel space. This space has access to the system hardware and provides all the core
functionalities to the system applications. A user can access this space only with the help
of system calls. Kernel space contains the kernel code, which are data structures that are
identical to all the processes that are running on the system. In kernel space, memory is
directly mapped to the physical memory.

User Space

The space that is allocated to the running applications is called *user space*. User space
consists of data, process data, and memory-mapped files. In user space, memory
mapping differs from one address space to another address space. The kernel supervises
the activities that a process needs to perform on the user space.

A kernel which has a different memory space for user services and kernel services is called a *microkernel*. In microkernels, users use the user space while the kernel uses the kernel space to perform system activities. The advantage of a microkernel is that a new service is easily created. The disadvantage is that it increases the execution time of the activity due to different address spaces.

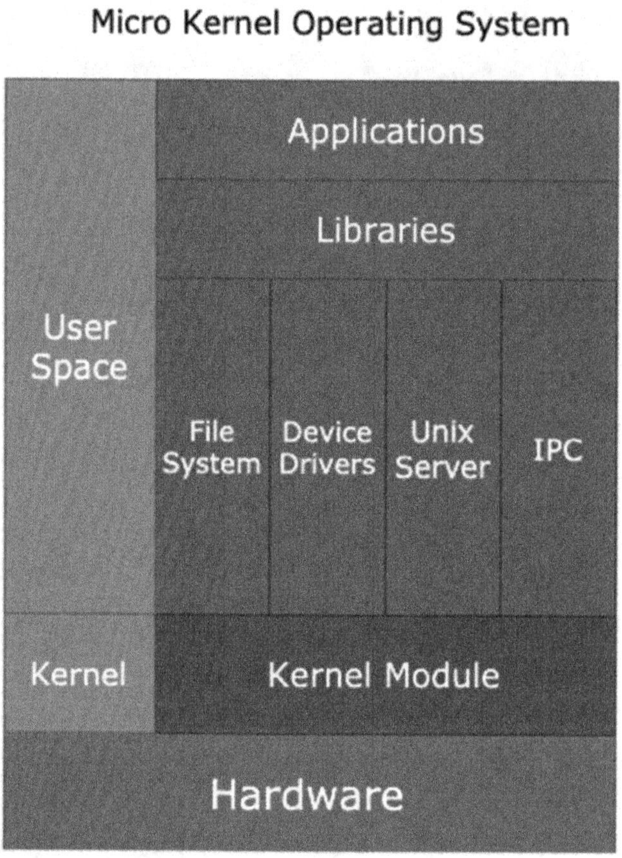

Figure 1-3. *Microkernel architecture*

Hybrid Kernels

A *hybrid kernel* is the combination of a monolithic kernel and a microkernel to improve the performance of the operating system. It takes the advantages of both kernels to improve the performance of the operating system.

Nanokernels

A *nanokernel* works on a nanosecond clock resolution. It is a very small and minimalistic kernel that performs an activity. It provides good hardware abstraction, but there is a lack of system services. The functionality of the kernel does not depend on IPC (interprocess communication).

Exokernels

An *exokernel* provides direct application-level management of the hardware resources. This kernel has limited functionality because of its small size. It allows you to perform application-level customization very easily. It is very interactive and efficient, but the disadvantage is its complex architecture and design.

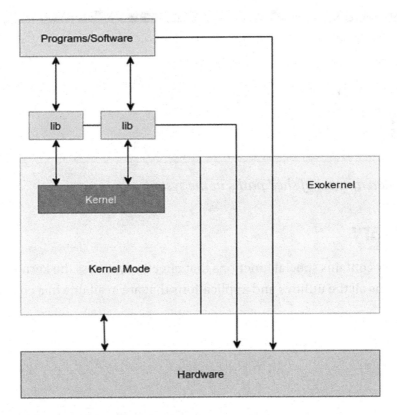

Figure 1-4. *Exokernel architecture*

Shell

A shell is a software program that executes other commands in a Unix-based operating system. The task of the shell is that it takes input from the user and performs the action based on the given input. By default, all Unix/Linux-based operating systems contain a bash shell. This shell hides the complexity of the kernel functionality from the users.

There are six types of shells.

- Z shell (zsh)

- POSIX shell (sh)

- Bash shell (bash)

- Korn shell (ksh)

- CShell (csh)

- TENEX C shell (tcsh)

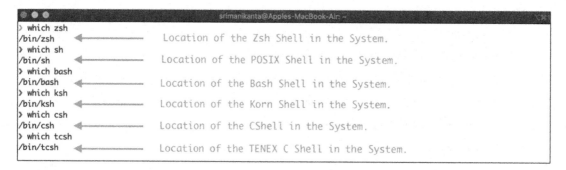

Figure 1-5. *Different types of shell paths in the system*

System Library

The system library contains special functions that effectively access the kernel's features. It contains all the utilities and applications that are available in a common operating system.

Linux Kernels vs. Other OS Kernels

Linux uses the monolithic kernel, whereas operating systems like Windows and macOS use the hybrid kernel. The performance of the Linux operating system is faster because it does not have the same address space for the applications and kernel. Since Linux uses the monolithic kernel, which is a core kernel that does not have any hybrid features, it makes Linux more advantageous than other operating systems. These monolithic kernel activities allow Linux to perform out-of-the-box system activities that other operating systems cannot.

Linux has a good package manager that downloads and sets up software very easily. This is not available on other operating systems. Homebrew is the "missing" package manager available for macOS that resolves this issue to some extent. There is no such kind of package manager to install software and set up easily on Windows.

In Linux, you can set up device drivers more easily other than on other operating systems. In Linux, the system calls are very fast and interactive.

The following are some simple reasons why using Linux is preferable to using Windows or macOS.

- Open source

- Flexibility

- Reliability

- Customization

- Security

- Good hardware support

Linux is open source so that developers can perform reverse engineering on the operating system's code, which helps developers build custom modules and modify the operating system. Operating systems like macOS X and Windows don't have an open source feature, which is why Linux is so popular among developers.

Introduction to Files

Files are commonly used to store data. The data in a file determines the file type. In general, there are five types of files available on any operating system.

- Text files

- Program files

- Binary files

- Special files

- General files

A file type is revealed by its extension. An image is a file that contains the most common extensions (.png, .jpg, .jpeg, .tiff, .gif, etc.). Files are maintained and managed by the *file system*, which is a hierarchical structure that stores the content in a structured format. These file structures are discussed in upcoming chapters. For now, let's discuss each file type.

Text File

A text file contains data that the reader can easily read. These files are created by the user or system-generated log files. There are many types of text files. Log files usually have the .log extension. The README.md file is a normal text file that uses markup language.

Program File

A program file contains a set of instructions written by the software developer to produce the software or application. There is no common extension for program files because there are multiple programming languages. The program file extension is based on the programming language in which the file content is written. The rules and syntax differ by programming language. The most common extensions are .c, .cpp, .java, .sh, and .bat. These program files become executable based on the requirements and usage. You can use any type of extension to perform the same task, but it is recommended to use the standard extension given by the ISO.

Binary File

A *binary file* contains information that is a combination of 0s and 1s. The information in a binary file is not human-readable or understandable. It is only understood by computers. Binary files are generally executable files. These files are generated by compiling a program file. You can convert a program file into an executable file; for example, when you compile a C program, it will generate an executable file.

Special File

A *special file* is implicitly created by a system process, or it is explicitly created by a programmer for a specific purpose. Examples of a special file include pipes and message queue files. Special files are explained in upcoming chapters.

Regular File

A *regular file* contains information on a photo, song, or video that is downloaded from the Internet or created by the user. The most common examples are images, audio, and videos.

File Handling Utilities

There are various built-in commands in Unix-like operating systems to handle the files on the operating system. These commands and utilities are executed from the terminal and are described next.

mkdir

Syntax → mkdir <dirname_with_Location>

   Explanation → mkdir stands for *make directory*. It creates a directory on an operating system. A directory is like a box that stores various types of files and other directories.

   Example → mkdir Linux

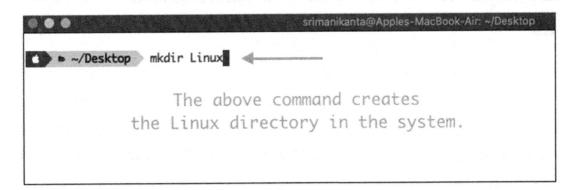

Figure 1-6. *mkdir command*

cd

Syntax ➔ cd <dirname>

Explanation ➔ cd stands for *change directory*. It changes the directory from the current directory to a specified directory with the help of a destination directory location.

Example ➔ cd Linux

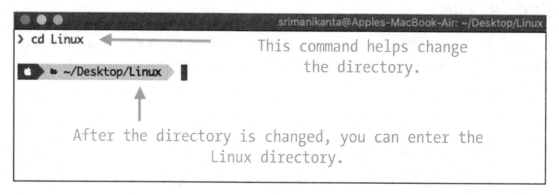

Figure 1-7. *cd command*

rmdir

Syntax ➔ rmdir <dirname>

Explanation ➔ rmdir deletes an empty directory. If you try to delete a non-empty directory with rmdir, an error is generated.

Example ➔ rmdir Linux

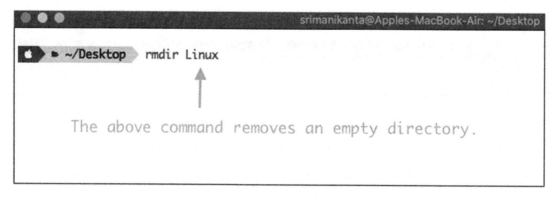

Figure 1-8. *rmdir command*

In Figure 1-9, a directory named MyFolder contains another directory named MyTemp; so, MyFolder is not empty. When the rmdir command is entered, the operating system simply throws an error saying that the directory is not empty.

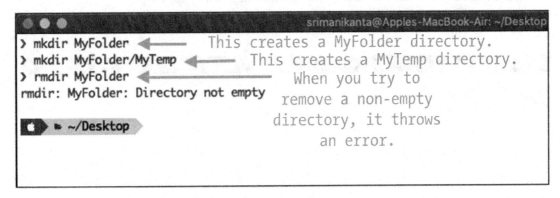

Figure 1-9. *rmdir command when trying to delete non-empty directory*

rm

Syntax → rm <filename/Directory Name>

Explanation → rm deletes the file directories in an operating system. Files are easily deleted with the rm command, but to delete directories, you need to add extra flags.

Example → rm filename

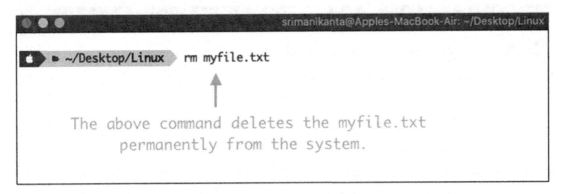

Figure 1-10. *rm command*

The following are options for the rm command.

Option ➔ -r

Syntax ➔ rm -r <dirname>

Explanation ➔ The command deletes a directory that is not empty.

Example ➔ $rm -r Linux

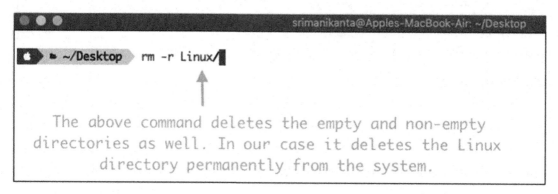

Figure 1-11. *rm command with -r option*

Option ➔ -f

Syntax ➔ rm -f <filename>

Explanation ➔ The command forcibly deletes a file.

Example ➔ rm -f Linux

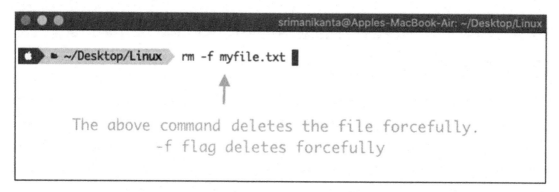

Figure 1-12. *rm command with -f option*

Note   If you want to forcibly delete a directory, use -f with the -r flag.

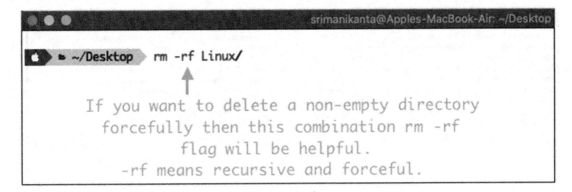

Figure 1-13. *rm command with -rf option*

touch

Syntax → touch <filename1> <filename2> ------ <filenamen>

Explanation → The touch command creates several empty files with 0 bytes each. This command is helpful when the user wants to create an empty file to use later.

Example → $touch file1 file2 file3

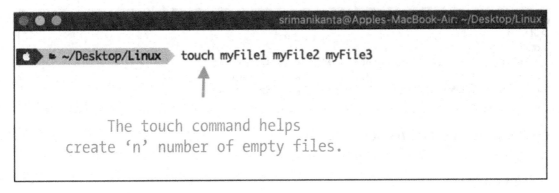

Figure 1-14. *touch command*

ls

Syntax → ls

Explanation → The ls command displays a list of files and directories.

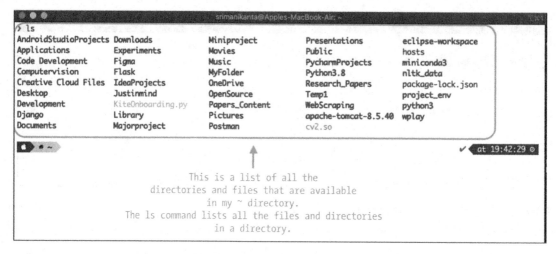

Figure 1-15. *ls command*

The following are some of the options for ls.

Option → -l

Syntax → ls -l

Explanation → This command displays a long list of files and directories.

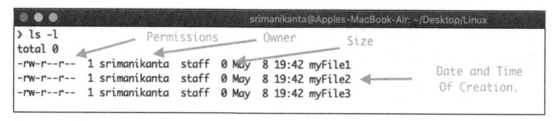

Figure 1-16. *ls command with -l option*

Option → -t

Syntax → ls -t

Explanation → This command sorts the files and directories according to the time of modification.

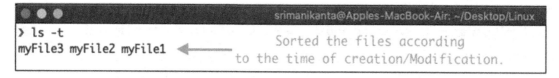

Figure 1-17. *ls command with -t option*

Option ➜ -a

Syntax ➜ ls -a

Explanation ➜ This command lists all the hidden files and directories. A hidden file is easily created with the **.** operator. A file or directory name that starts with **.** is a hidden directory or file.

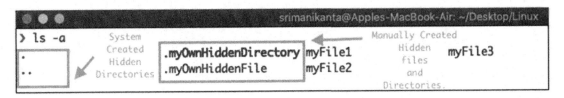

Figure 1-18. *ls command with -a option*

cat

Syntax ➜ cat > <filename>

    Explanation ➜ The cat command creates a file with specified content. You can write content as required with this command. After the content is written, you exit from the command by pressing Ctrl+D.

    Example ➜ cat > file1

```
Hello World…! This is Sri Manikanta. Happy Learning
^d
```

Figure 1-19. *cat command*

head

Syntax ➜ head <filename>

    Explanation ➜ The head command displays the lines at the beginning of the file.

    Example 1 ➜ head myContent.txt

    Explanation ➜ The default command displays the first ten lines of the file.

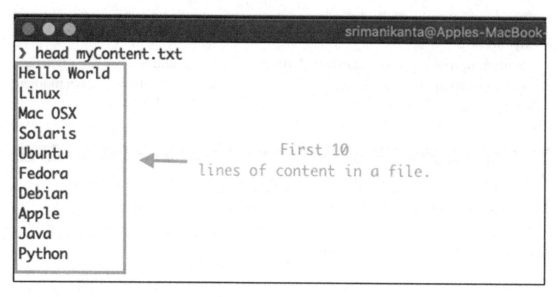

Figure 1-20. *head command*

Example 2 head -5 file2

Explanation ➔ The flag number that is added before the file name displays the first *n* lines of the file.

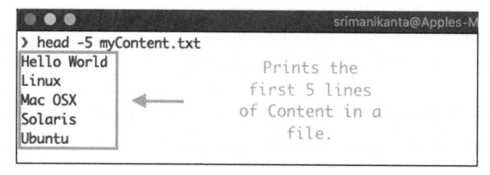

Figure 1-21. *head command with -number option*

Example3 ➔ head -c42 file3

Explanation ➔ The -c flag displays up to *n* number of the first characters in a file.

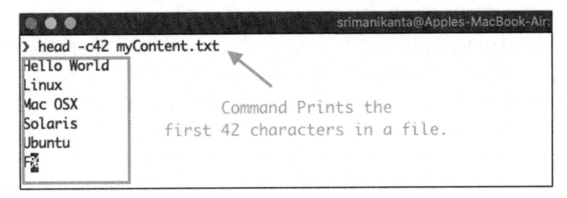

Figure 1-22. *head command with -number of characters option*

tail

Syntax → `tail <filename>`

   Explanation → The `tail` command displays the content at the end of a file.

   Example1 → `tail myContent.txt`

   Explanation → The default command displays the last ten lines of the file.

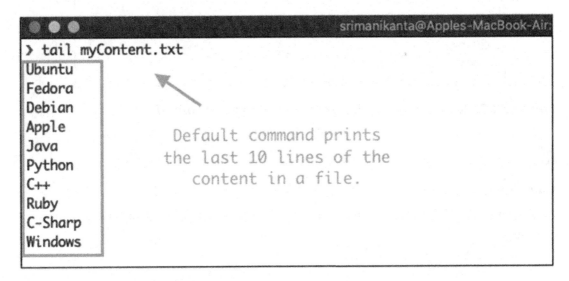

Figure 1-23. *tail command*

   Example2 → `tail -5 myContent.txt`

   Explanation → The flag number before the file name displays the last *n* lines of a file.

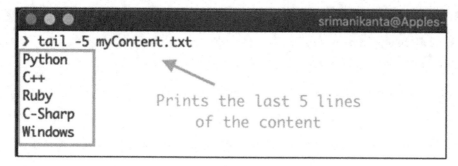

Figure 1-24. *tail command with -number option*

Example3 ➜ $tail -c42 file3

Explanation ➜ The -c flag displays up to *n* number of characters in a file.

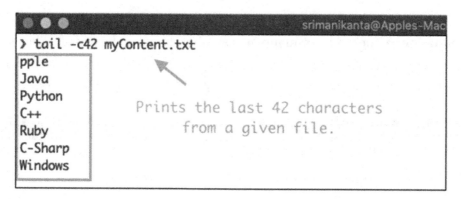

Figure 1-25. *tail command with -number of characters option*

nl

Syntax ➜ nl <filename>

    Explanation ➜ The nl command displays the content of a file along with the line numbers.

    Example ➜ nl myContent.txt

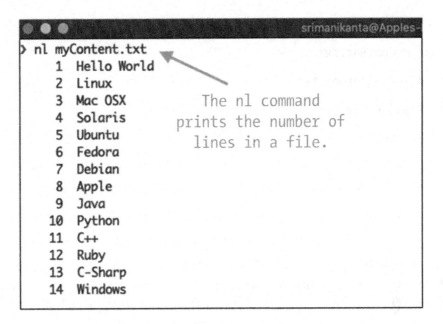

Figure 1-26. nl command

WC

Syntax → wc [options] filenames

Explanation → The wc command displays the newline count, word count, bytes, and the number of characters in a file, as specified by the file arguments.

Options

- wc -l: Prints the number of lines in a file.

- wc -w: Prints the number of words in a file.

- wc -c: Displays the number of bytes in a file.

- wc -m: Prints the number of characters in a file.

Examples

- wc myContent.txt

    14 16 98 myContent.txt

- wc -l myContent.txt

    14 myContent.txt

- `wc -w myContent.txt`

  `16 myContent.txt`

- `wc -c myContent.txt`

  `98 myContent.txt`

- `wc -m myContent.txt`

  `98 myContent.txt`

copy

Syntax ➔ `cp <source_file> <destination_file>`

Explanation ➔ The `cp` command copies data from one file to another or to a directory. To copy content from directories, you need to use the recursive flag, which is `-r`.

Example1 ➔ `cp file1 file2`

Explanation: This command copies the contents of file1 to file2. If file2 does not exist, it is created.

Example2 ➔ `cp file1 file2 Files/`

Explanation: This command copies multiple files into a single directory. The directory must exist.

ulimit

Syntax ➔ `ulimit`

Explanation ➔ `ulimit` stands for *user limit*. It signifies the largest file that can be created by the user in the file system.

File Permission Commands

File permission commands are very useful for changing the permissions of a file or directory. These commands grant or revoke access rights, such as read, write, or execute to a particular file.

chmod

Syntax ➔ chmod [who] [+/-/=] [permissions] <filename>

Explanation ➔ Unix grants permissions for files and directories. You can change permissions using the chmod command.

In the syntax, who can be any four of the following items.

- u stands for *user*. The user is the owner of the file or directory. The person who creates the file or directory is considered the user or owner.

- g stands for *group*. A group consists of multiple users who have the same access permission for a file.

- o stands for *others*. This is any user who has access to a file but did not create the file and does not belong in a user group. It is generally considered setting the permissions for the world to use the data.

- a stands for *all*. It includes all types of users (i.e., owner, groups, and others to use the file data.

  [+/-/=] can be classified as

- + adds the permissions to a file or directory

- - removes the permissions to a file or directory

- = instructs chmod to add the specified permissions and take away all others, if present

Permissions include any of the following three categories in a Linux/Unix file system.

Read

Read access allows you to view the content of a file or list the files in a directory. With this permission, you are not able to edit or modify any content in the file. You are not able to add or remove any file from the directory with this access.

Write

Write permission allows you to modify the content in a file. Write permissions allow you to add, remove, delete, and rename a file or directory.

Execute

To execute a program in Linux, you need to set the execute permissions to the file. The following are examples.

- `chmod +rw myContents.txt` gives read and write permissions to all.

- `chmod go-x myContents.txt` takes away execute permission from groups and others.

- `chmod ug+r, go-w myContents.txt` gives read permission to users and groups and takes away write permission to groups and others.

- `chmod go=w, u=rwx myContents.txt` removes all existing permissions and replaces them with write permission for groups and others and read, write, and execute permissions for the owner of `myContents.txt`.

You can change the permissions of certain files and directories in an operating system. This method is a little tricky for beginners in the Linux environment. There is a better and easier way to change the permissions for a file or directory. It is done with weights.

Changing Permissions with Weights

Instead of using u/g/o and +/-/=, you can use weights. It is an octal representation.

- Read: (4)

- Write: (2)

- Execute: (1).

The weight for read access is 4.
The weight for write access is 2.
The weight for execute access is 1.

Table 1-1. *File Permission Modes*

Octal	Binary	File Mode
0	000	---
1	001	--x
2	010	-w-
3	011	-wx
4	100	r--
5	101	r-x
6	110	rw-
7	111	rwx

Here are some examples.

- chmod 754 myContents.txt assigns permissions as follows: rwxr-xr--

- chmod 777 myContents.txt assigns permissions as follows: rwxrwxrwx

- chmod 654 myContents.txt assigns permissions as follows: rw-r-xr--

- chmod 557 myContents.txt assigns permissions as follows: r-xr-xrwx

This octal representation based on weights is very easy to understand. These commands are mainly used by system administrators and Linux power users to change permissions.

To get file types and the access permission, you can use the ls -l command, which is a long list command in Linux/Unix.

Process Utilities

Process

A process is a program under execution. You can call it as an instance of a program. To get a clear view of a process, let's look at an example. Suppose that when you open your terminal to create a file with data in it, you use the cat command, which creates, writes, concatenates file content, and prints to the standard output. In this case, you are creating a normal text file and writing content in it. When a user performs this action automatically, a process is created. Whenever you assign tasks to the operating system, the OS automatically creates a process for it.

Every process has unique properties.

- The process has a unique process ID that is generated by the operating system.

- The task of each process independent.

- A process can have multiple threads.

There are two types of processes: foreground and background.

Foreground Process

A process that depends on input from the user is called a *foreground process*. Initially, every process created by the user is a foreground process.

The creation of a file and entering data into it is a good example of the foreground process.

Background Process

A *background process* runs independently of the shell. The biggest advantage of a background process is that you can multitask. If the background process requires user input, it waits until the input is provided.

The following are two examples.

- Listing all the files in a directory with extensions.

- Executing a program that does not depend on user input. The best example of these kinds of programs is stress tests in Competitive programming.

Process Commands

The types of processes are discussed in the upcoming chapters. Let's dive into the process utilities that monitor the processing activity in a system.

ps

Syntax ➔ ps

Explanation ➔ The ps (process) command reports information on current running processes, outputting to standard output.

Example

1) **ps**

```
> ps                  Unique Process ID
   PID TTY              TIME CMD              Actively Running Processes in my System.
  1233 ttys001      0:00.04 /Applications/iTerm.app/Contents/MacOS/iTerm2 --server login -fp srimanikanta
  1235 ttys001      0:01.54 -zsh
  1241 ttys001      0:00.01 zsh -dfxc \012         exec >&4\012          echo $$\012          /Users/srimanikanta/
  1242 ttys001      0:00.12 /Users/srimanikanta/.oh-my-zsh/custom/themes/powerlevel10k/gitstatus/bin/gitstatu
```

Figure 1-27. ps command

The result contains four columns of information.

- PID: A unique process number that is generated by the operating system

- TTY: The name of the console that the user is logged into

- TIME: The amount of CPU time (in minutes and seconds) that the process has been running

- CMD: The name of the command that launched the process

Options

Option ➔ -e
  Syntax ➔ ps -e
  Explanation ➔ The -e flag lists all the processes that are running on the system.

Figure 1-28. *ps command with -e option*

top

Syntax ➜ top

   Explanation ➜ The top command displays all the top processes in the system. This command also periodically updates the process information.

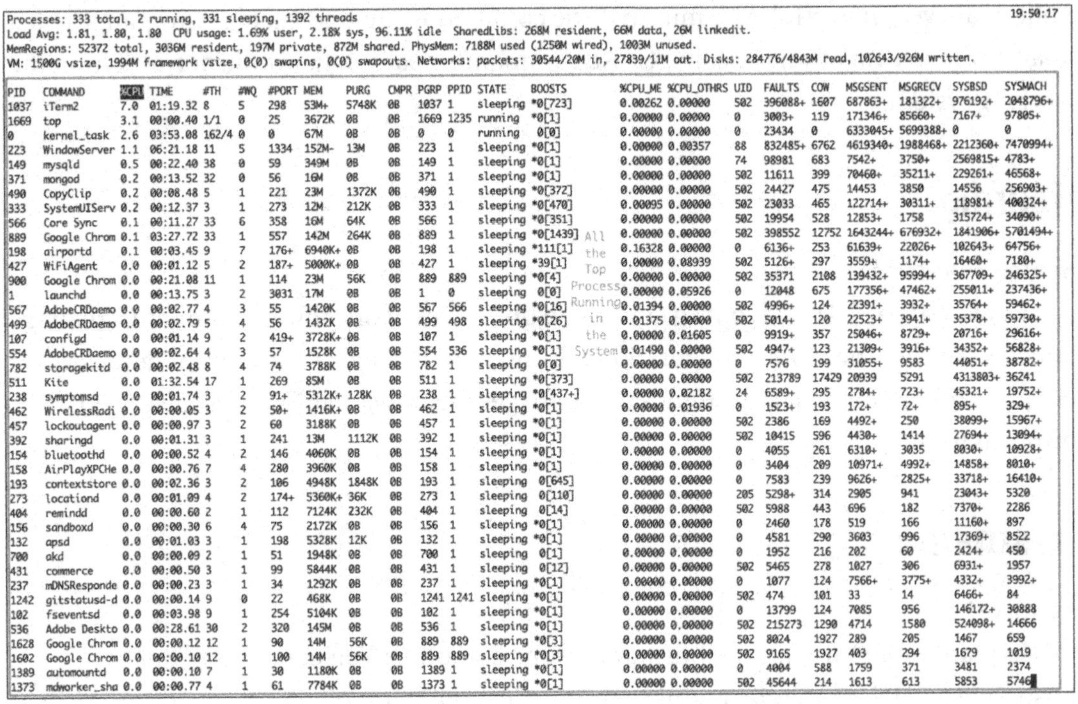

Figure 1-29. *top command*

kill

Syntax →

```
kill -s [signal_name] pid
kill -l [exit_status]
kill -signal_name pid
kill -signal_number pid
```

Explanation → The kill command manually terminates a signal or process.

Exit status → The kill utility exits at 0 on success and >0 if an error occurs.
This command and its exit status are discussed in upcoming chapters.

Network Utilities

Network tools are needed to communicate with the network systems. Network utilities
directly communicate through a connection with remote systems and servers via the
IP address. These network commands also analyze the overall network data. Network

utilities are very powerful. The minimalistic commands run and execute programs to analyze the network traffic locally. These commands analyze the whole network from the working system.

ifconfig

Syntax ➔ `ifconfig`

    Explanation ➔ The `ifconfig` command obtains network configuration information and lets you view network configuration information. It displays the current network adapter configuration. It determines if you are getting transmit (TX) or receive (RX) errors as well.

hostname

Syntax ➔ `hostname`

    Explanation ➔ It finds the hostname of the computer. You can change this hostname by making modifications to the system configuration files.

```
> hostname
Apples-MacBook-Air.local  ◄──────    Hostname of my Machine.
```

Figure 1-30. *hostname command*

netstat

Syntax ➔ `netstat`

    Explanation ➔ The `netstat` command identifies the open and closed ports in a network. It determines all the active network connections, routing tables information, interface statistics, and so forth. This command is very useful and versatile in finding a connection to and from the host.

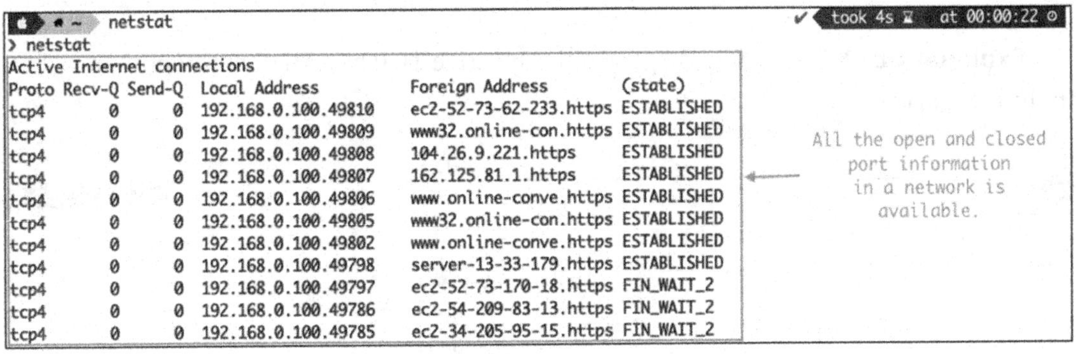

```
netstat                                                                    ✔ took 4s ⌛ at 00:00:22 ⊙
> netstat
Active Internet connections
Proto Recv-Q Send-Q  Local Address         Foreign Address       (state)
tcp4       0      0  192.168.0.100.49810   ec2-52-73-62-233.https ESTABLISHED
tcp4       0      0  192.168.0.100.49809   www32.online-con.https ESTABLISHED
tcp4       0      0  192.168.0.100.49808   104.26.9.221.https     ESTABLISHED
tcp4       0      0  192.168.0.100.49807   162.125.81.1.https     ESTABLISHED
tcp4       0      0  192.168.0.100.49806   www.online-conve.https ESTABLISHED
tcp4       0      0  192.168.0.100.49805   www32.online-con.https ESTABLISHED
tcp4       0      0  192.168.0.100.49802   www.online-conve.https ESTABLISHED
tcp4       0      0  192.168.0.100.49798   server-13-33-179.https ESTABLISHED
tcp4       0      0  192.168.0.100.49797   ec2-52-73-170-18.https FIN_WAIT_2
tcp4       0      0  192.168.0.100.49786   ec2-54-209-83-13.https FIN_WAIT_2
tcp4       0      0  192.168.0.100.49785   ec2-34-205-95-15.https FIN_WAIT_2
```

All the open and closed port information in a network is available.

Figure 1-31. *netstat command*

Syntax ➔ netstat -g

Explanation ➔ The -g flag determines all the multicast groups subscribed to the current working host machine.

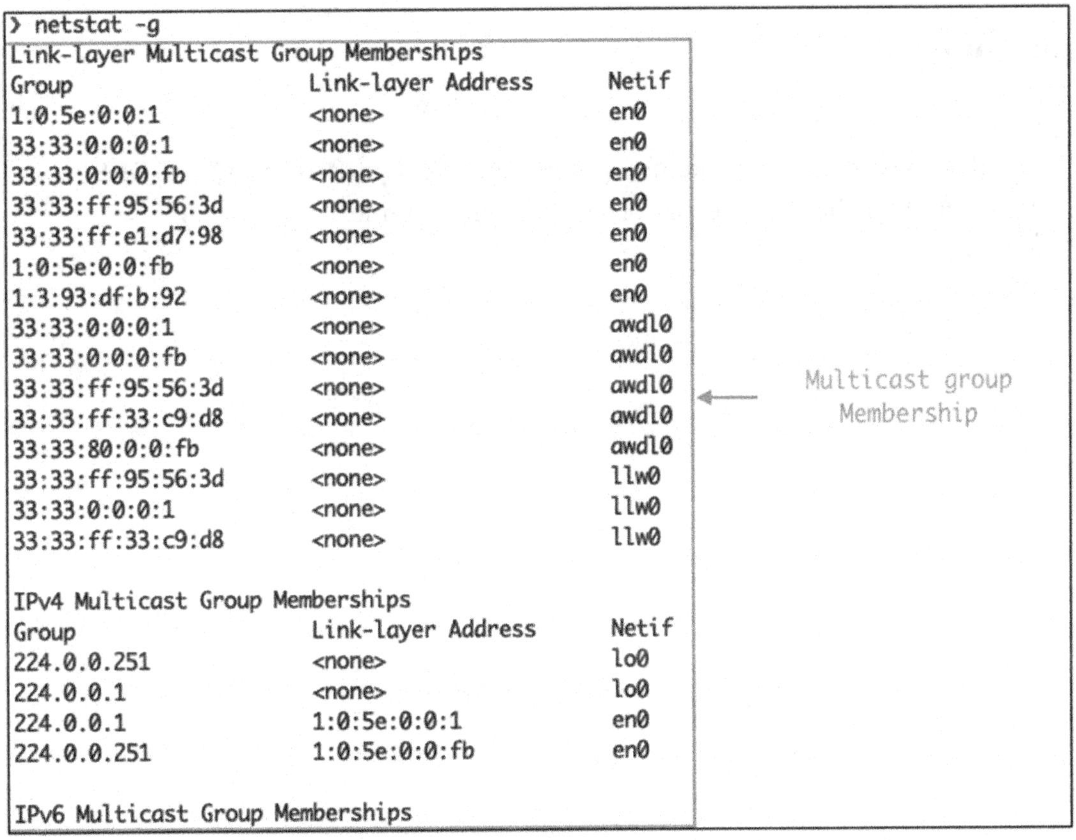

```
> netstat -g
Link-layer Multicast Group Memberships
Group                   Link-layer Address      Netif
1:0:5e:0:0:1            <none>                  en0
33:33:0:0:0:1           <none>                  en0
33:33:0:0:0:fb          <none>                  en0
33:33:ff:95:56:3d       <none>                  en0
33:33:ff:e1:d7:98       <none>                  en0
1:0:5e:0:0:fb           <none>                  en0
1:3:93:df:b:92          <none>                  en0
33:33:0:0:0:1           <none>                  awdl0
33:33:0:0:0:fb          <none>                  awdl0
33:33:ff:95:56:3d       <none>                  awdl0
33:33:ff:33:c9:d8       <none>                  awdl0
33:33:80:0:0:fb         <none>                  awdl0
33:33:ff:95:56:3d       <none>                  llw0
33:33:0:0:0:1           <none>                  llw0
33:33:ff:33:c9:d8       <none>                  llw0

IPv4 Multicast Group Memberships
Group                   Link-layer Address      Netif
224.0.0.251             <none>                  lo0
224.0.0.1               <none>                  lo0
224.0.0.1               1:0:5e:0:0:1            en0
224.0.0.251             1:0:5e:0:0:fb           en0

IPv6 Multicast Group Memberships
```

Multicast group Membership

Figure 1-32. *netstat command with -g option*

Syntax → netstat -a

Explanation → The -a flag displays all the active TCP and UDP connections, including servers.

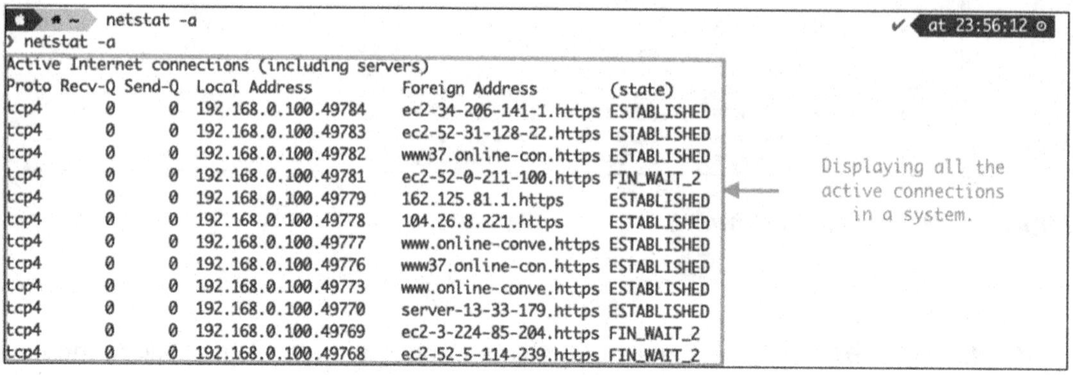

Figure 1-33. *netstat command with -a option*

nslookup

Syntax → nslookup netflix.com

Explanation → nslookup stands for *name server lookup*. It troubleshoots DNS servers. It finds all the IP addresses for a given domain name.

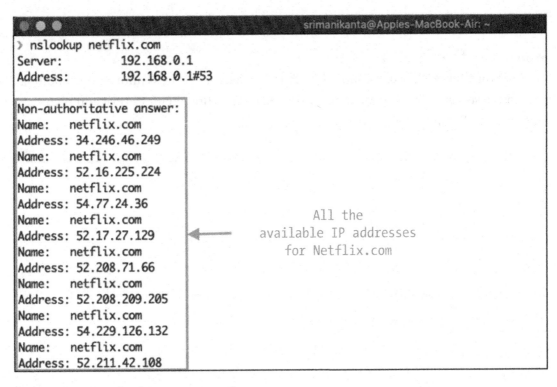

Figure 1-34. nslookup command

traceroute

Syntax → traceroute netflix.com

    Explanation → traceroute shows the number of hops and response times to make a connection with a remote system or website. This command simply traces all the activities between the remote server and the local system.

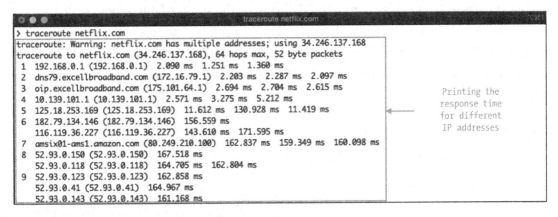

Figure 1-35. traceroute command

host

Syntax ➜ host netflix.com

Explanation ➜ The host command identifies network address information about the remote servers connected to a network. The information includes IPv4 and IPv6 addresses and mail server information.

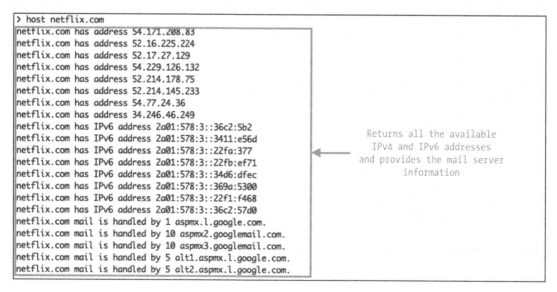

Figure 1-36. *host command*

ping

Syntax ➜ ping sriindugroup.org

Explanation ➜ The ping command determines the status of the remote system or server. If the remote server is up and running, you receive packets of data from it; otherwise, you get a Request Timeout message. In some cases, the server is up but configured to not respond to ping requests (this is actually very common, to avoid ICMP DDOS attacks).

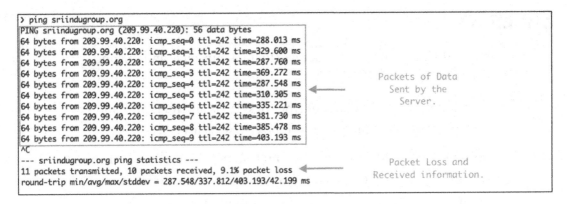

```
⟩ ping sriindugroup.org
PING sriindugroup.org (209.99.40.220): 56 data bytes
64 bytes from 209.99.40.220: icmp_seq=0 ttl=242 time=288.013 ms
64 bytes from 209.99.40.220: icmp_seq=1 ttl=242 time=329.600 ms
64 bytes from 209.99.40.220: icmp_seq=2 ttl=242 time=287.760 ms
64 bytes from 209.99.40.220: icmp_seq=3 ttl=242 time=369.272 ms
64 bytes from 209.99.40.220: icmp_seq=4 ttl=242 time=287.548 ms
64 bytes from 209.99.40.220: icmp_seq=5 ttl=242 time=310.305 ms
64 bytes from 209.99.40.220: icmp_seq=6 ttl=242 time=335.221 ms
64 bytes from 209.99.40.220: icmp_seq=7 ttl=242 time=381.730 ms
64 bytes from 209.99.40.220: icmp_seq=8 ttl=242 time=385.478 ms
64 bytes from 209.99.40.220: icmp_seq=9 ttl=242 time=403.193 ms
^C
--- sriindugroup.org ping statistics ---
11 packets transmitted, 10 packets received, 9.1% packet loss
round-trip min/avg/max/stddev = 287.548/337.812/403.193/42.199 ms
```

Packets of Data
Sent by the
Server.

Packet Loss and
Received information.

Figure 1-37. *ping command*

dig

Syntax ➔ dig netflix.com

Explanation ➔ dig stands for *domain information groper*. It queries DNS-related information to obtain all types of record information.

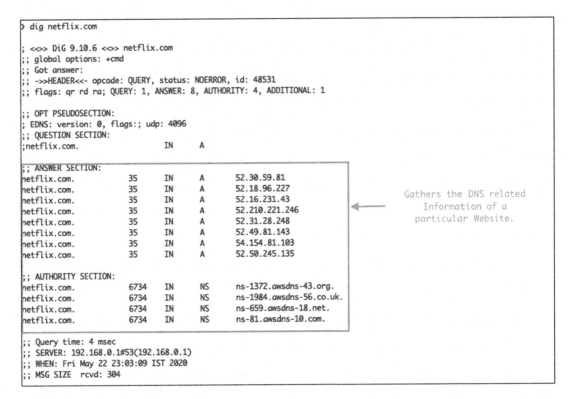

```
⟩ dig netflix.com

; <<>> DiG 9.10.6 <<>> netflix.com
;; global options: +cmd
;; Got answer:
;; ->>HEADER<<- opcode: QUERY, status: NOERROR, id: 48531
;; flags: qr rd ra; QUERY: 1, ANSWER: 8, AUTHORITY: 4, ADDITIONAL: 1

;; OPT PSEUDOSECTION:
; EDNS: version: 0, flags:; udp: 4096
;; QUESTION SECTION:
;netflix.com.            IN     A

;; ANSWER SECTION:
netflix.com.       35    IN     A      52.30.59.81
netflix.com.       35    IN     A      52.18.96.227
netflix.com.       35    IN     A      52.16.231.43
netflix.com.       35    IN     A      52.210.221.246
netflix.com.       35    IN     A      52.31.28.248
netflix.com.       35    IN     A      52.49.81.143
netflix.com.       35    IN     A      54.154.81.103
netflix.com.       35    IN     A      52.50.245.135

;; AUTHORITY SECTION:
netflix.com.       6734  IN     NS     ns-1372.awsdns-43.org.
netflix.com.       6734  IN     NS     ns-1984.awsdns-56.co.uk.
netflix.com.       6734  IN     NS     ns-659.awsdns-18.net.
netflix.com.       6734  IN     NS     ns-81.awsdns-10.com.

;; Query time: 4 msec
;; SERVER: 192.168.0.1#53(192.168.0.1)
;; WHEN: Fri May 22 23:03:09 IST 2020
;; MSG SIZE  rcvd: 304
```

Gathers the DNS related
Information of a
particular Website.

Figure 1-38. *dig command*

Summary

- In this chapter, you were introduced to the Linux environment and architecture.

- You learned about the different types of kernels and their pros and cons. File handling utilities in the Linux OS were also discussed.

- Processes and the different types of built-in utilities that are available were explained. There was a discussion on how network utilities identify and extract various kinds of information.

- By the end of this chapter, you should be able to work with the Linux environment.

CHAPTER 2

Multithreading in C

Multithreading is a program's ability to execute multiple threads simultaneously to maximize the utilization of the CPU. Multithreading helps achieve concurrency. Concurrenscy is parallelly executing multiple threads at the same time. In this chapter, you learn about the following topics with practical coding.

- Introduction to threads and thread behavior

- The difference between threads and processes

- Concurrency

- Parallelism

- Introduction to multithreading

- Importance of multithreading

- Multithreading API in C

- Creating multithreading programs in C

- Practical examples of multithreading

- Multithreading use cases

Introduction to Threads

A thread is a lightweight process that shares a common address space with the owner process. Threads are very helpful in performing parallel programming tasks to achieve concurrency. Applications such as video editing software, web servers, online conferencing software, and text editors use multiple threads to do their jobs more efficiently. A thread is a small segment in a process, as shown in Figure 2-1.

© Sri Manikanta Palakollu 2021
S. M. Palakollu, *Practical System Programming with C*, https://doi.org/10.1007/978-1-4842-6321-1_2

Thread Program

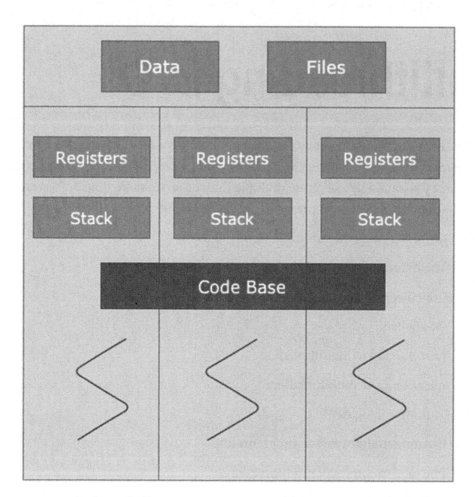

Figure 2-1. *Multithreaded process*

Every thread has a program counter and stack space for storing an activity. The usage of threads greater benefits than processes. The following are the main advantages of using threads.

- They are easy to create and handle.

- They achieve concurrency in parallel programming.

- They reduce context switching time in an operating system.

- They can effectively utilize multiprocessor architecture.

- Thread communication is much faster than process communication because threads share common address space.

- They increase the overall performance of a system.

Thread Classification

Threads are classified into two types: user-level threads and kernel-level threads.

User-Level Threads

The user creates user-level threads with thread libraries rather than system calls. These threads are independent of the kernel. The user does thread management according to his needs and requirements. For example, creating a thread is done by the user. The thread library performs thread management in the user space. It doesn't depend on the operating system's system calls.

The creation of user-level threads is much faster than kernel-level threads. User-level threads don't depend on hardware utility. Context switching is easier with user-level threads because it is done in the user space with a thread library. But, when it comes to kernel-level threads, context switching is done in a kernel space. In a kernel space, there might be a situation where more than one thread is in an active state at a particular time. If the multiple threads are in a kernel space, then it takes some extra time for context switching.

In general, context switching in user-level threads is faster than in kernel-level threads, but this may change based on the situation. User-level threads are represented by a program counter. Some good examples of user-level threads are POSIX threads and Java threads.

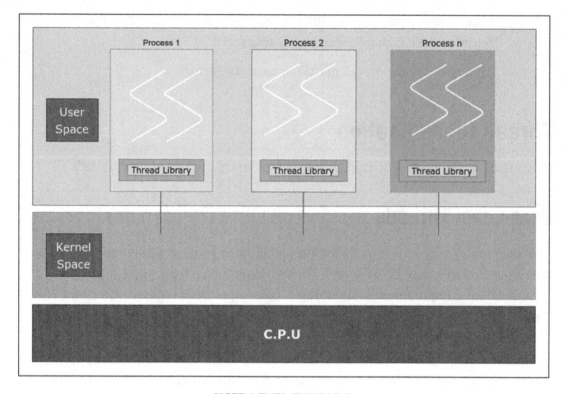

USER LEVEL THREADS

Figure 2-2. *User-level threads working mechanism*

The following are the advantages of user-level threads.

- They are easy to create.

- They are platform-independent, which means they can run on any operating system.

- Kernel-mode privileges are not required for thread switching.

- Context switching is very easy for an operating system.

- They don't depend upon the system hardware.

The following are the disadvantages of user-level threads.

- Multiprocessing is very difficult because it is independent of the kernel. When you want to perform a multiprocessing task in an operating system, kernel support is required to execute the task. This is impossible with these threads.

- They require nonblocking I/O calls; otherwise, the entire process may be blocked in the kernel.

Kernel-Level Threads

Kernel-level threads are created by the operating system directly. The kernel does thread management with a thread table that helps the kernel monitor all the activities done by a thread in the system. Some good examples of kernel-level threads are Win32 and Solaris.

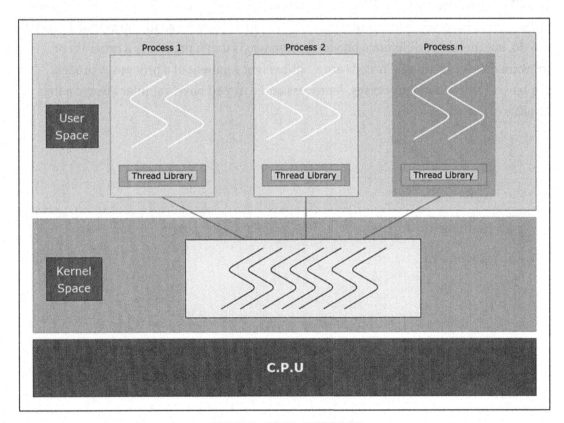

KERNEL LEVEL THREADS

Figure 2-3. *Kernel-level threads working mechanism*

The following are the advantages of kernel-level threads.

- Multiprocessing is done very easily.

- They work on the blocking I/O protocol.

The following are the disadvantages of kernel-level threads.

- They are slow and inefficient compared to user-level threads.

- They are very hard to create and manage.

- Multiple switching is required to transfer control from one thread to another thread.

Threads vs. Processes

Even though threads are small segments inside a process, there are differences between threads and processes in terms of parameters. A thread can do all the tasks that a process can do, but the major difference between these two is that a process is a program or software that is executing. Threads are a lightweight segment of a process. A process can have multiple child processes. A process and a thread have a similar life cycle that consists of five stages.

1. New

2. Ready

3. Wait

4. Running

5. Terminated

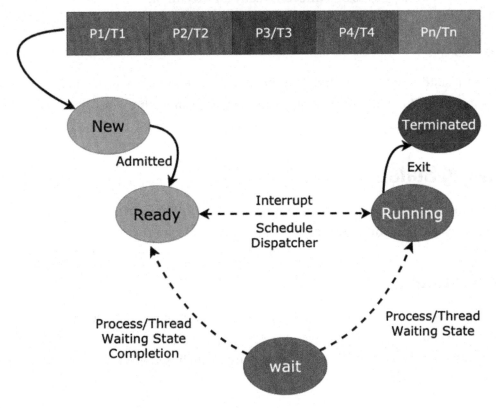

Figure 2-4. *Process and thread life cycle*

The diagram highlights the five stages of the thread and process life cycle. Now let's discuss each stage.

New State

In the new state, a new process or thread is created and added to the queue. If it is a process, it is created by a system call based on user input and then added to the queue. Generally, a process is created with fork(). Threads are created based on the programmer's code and added to the queue explicitly. In a new state, the thread or process has been created, but it is not running.

Ready State

In the ready state, a process or a thread is ready for execution.

Wait State

In the wait state, a process or thread has been blocked for some reason and for some amount of time. When it resumes, it goes to the ready state; otherwise, the thread/process is terminated.

Running State

The running state describes the execution of the process/thread. In this state, if the sleep method is called on a thread/process, it goes to the wait state.

Terminated

When the execution of a process or thread has been completed, it moves to the termination state.

The differences between threads and processes are based on certain characteristics, as shown in Table 2-1.

Table 2-1. *Relationship Between Threads and Processes*

Characteristics	Threads	Processes
Definition	A thread is a lightweight segment that is a part of a process.	A process is any program or software that is executing.
Creation Time	Threads usually take very little time to create since they are lightweight.	A process requires more time to create because the process is heavier than a thread.
Termination Time	A thread requires little time to terminate because of its simple nature.	A process requires more time to terminate because of its complex structure.

(*continued*)

Table 2-1. (*continued*)

Characteristics	Threads	Processes
Resource Usage	A thread needs a minimal number of resources to do its task.	A process uses more resources than threads.
Memory Sharing	Threads share memory with other threads based on the task to perform.	All the processes created in an operating system are isolated. They don't communicate with any other processes.
Communication	Threads can communicate with other threads within the same process more effectively than a process.	Processes are less efficient than threads.
Context Switching	A thread requires less time for context switching in an OS. It is less expensive.	A process requires more time for context switching because of its heaviness. It is more expensive in processes.
Management	Threads do not depend on any OS system calls.	A process depends on system calls.

Introduction to Multithreading

In your operating system, generally, you can perform multiple tasks at the same time. For example, listening to music on iTunes while writing code in a text editor is considered multitasking. In multitasking, computer applications execute different tasks simultaneously. Multithreading is very similar to multitasking, but the key difference is that multitasking works on the process, whereas multithreading works on threads.

Multitasking Architecture

When the CPU executes multiple tasks with the process by switching between activities in a minimal amount of time, multitasking enables users to interact with several applications at the same time. In multitasking architecture, the execution of a task is done by the processor by sharing memory space and allocation for each task.

In the architecture shown in Figure 2-5, an operating system is running four different applications (i.e., a text editor, iTunes, Google Chrome, and Keynote software). Consider a situation where the user is writing code using a text editor while listening to music on iTunes. He has a list of features that need to be implemented, which is available in a Keynote file, so he opens the Keynote application. In the middle of development, he wants to refer to official documentation regarding the application, so he opens Google Chrome. Four applications are running parallel on his operating system. This situation is called *multitasking*.

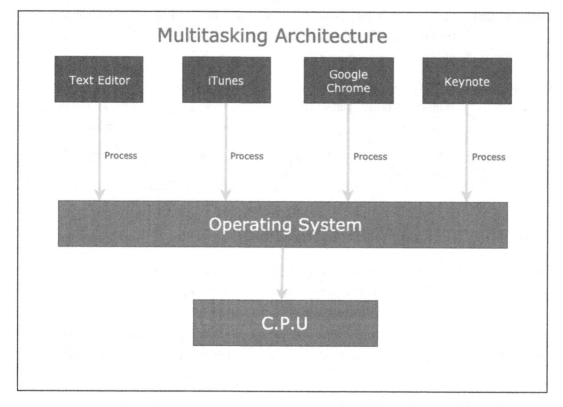

Figure 2-5. *Multitasking architecture*

Multithreading Architecture

In a multithreading architecture, a single process creates multiple threads to execute a task. In this architecture, common memory space and allocation is shared by all the threads. A multithreading architecture occurs within a process based on multiple threads.

Let's consider a situation in which a user is writing code in Visual Studio Code (a.k.a. VS Code). To develop code in VS Code, the operating system creates a single process for that task. A process creates multiple threads to effectively execute a task. A new thread is created for each of the following: when you open an integrated terminal in VS Code, when you open IntelliSense to write code, and when you format the code. In multithreading, some threads communicate with each other based on the situation. So, a thread is created to perform a task more effectively and without any lags during its execution.

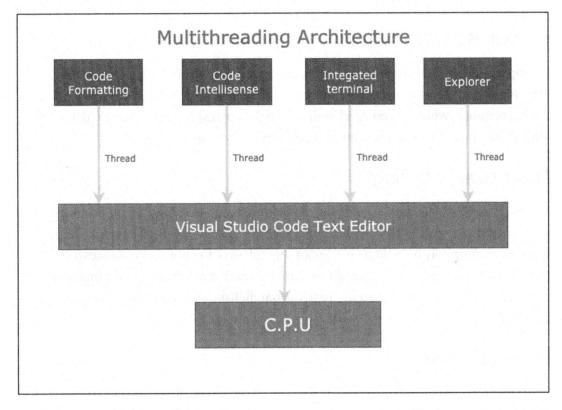

Figure 2-6. *Multithreading architecture*

Importance of Multithreading

A program executing a task with a single thread is not always effective, especially for video editing software, code editors, and so forth. To use powerful applications that have many tasks to do simultaneously within an application, then multithreading is very helpful.

High-level programming languages like C, C++, Java, and Python have a single thread by default—without creating anything. In the C language, the main function creates a single thread in the background by default; it works as a background thread, and it does its job as assigned by the compiler. Executing higher-order tasks with a single thread is not efficient, which leads to the need for multithreading.

The importance of multithreading in modern application development is due to its advantages over a single-threaded architecture. Multithreading architecture has many benefits, which are discussed next.

Efficient Resource Sharing

An application that executes a task may require common resources to share among multiple threads. This is done with standard techniques, such as message passing and shared memory (which are covered in upcoming chapters), which are very efficient in multithreading because of the common memory address space.

Application Scalability

Multithreading increases the scalability of the application because the application's subactivities are easily performed with multiple threads. For instance, a single-threaded application runs only on a single processor regardless of the number of processors. But a multithreaded application utilizes the multiple cores that are available in a machine. So, a multithreaded application can increase the parallelism in an operating system that has multiple core CPUs.

Responsiveness

Multithreading operations are performed in an application. All the internal threads work together to provide efficiency and a good user experience by increasing the responsiveness of the application.

Efficient Memory Utilization

In a multithreading environment, there is no need to create a separate memory for each thread. All threads share the same address space, so they use the memory effectively without creating new allocation spaces.

Efficient CPU Utilization

The creation of multiple threads within a process to execute a single application task increases speed and performance. Threads within a process utilize the improved CPU resources to perform the assigned task. Because threads use resources that are allocated by the process, indirectly, they are using better CPU resources, which results in efficient CPU utilization.

Concurrency

Concurrency is a mechanism that decreases the response time of the system by using a single processing unit. In concurrency, a major task is divided into subtasks that execute simultaneously but not at the same time. A good example of concurrency is having multiple applications, like a Chrome browser, a video editor, and iTunes running at the same time in an operating system.

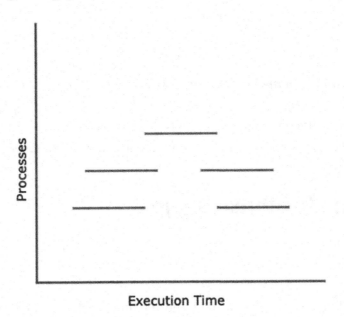

Figure 2-7. *Concurrency mechanism process execution time*

In Figure 2-7, five processes are executing simultaneously but not at the same time. You can observe the gap between the process executions. Concurrency creates an illusion that all processes are running simultaneously at the same time, but concurrency hides the latency time between process executions.

Parallelism

Parallelism is a mechanism that increases computational speed by using multiple processors. In parallelism, tasks execute simultaneously and at the same time. A good example of parallelism is running a video editor that has many tasks to perform simultaneously.

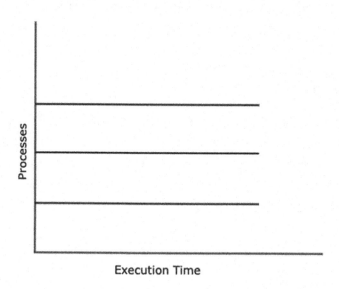

Figure 2-8. *Parallelism mechanism process execution time*

In Figure 2-8, all the processes are executing simultaneously and at the same time. This simultaneous execution results in an increase in the system's speed.

Support of Multithreading in C

The C programming language does not have built-in library support for multithreaded programming. Even though C is a general-purpose programming language that is widely used in embedded systems, system programming, and so forth, some vendors have developed libraries that deal with multithreading to achieve parallelism and concurrency.

The library to develop portable multithreaded applications is pthread.h; that is, the POSIX thread library. POSIX stands for *portable operating system interface*. POSIX threads are lightweight and designed to be very easy to implement. The pthread.h library is an external third-party library that helps you effectively do tasks.

Note   You can develop multithreaded programs with the pthread.h library in all Unix-based operating systems but not for Windows. If you want to develop an application that works on Windows, the windows.h library is very effective for multithreading-supported Windows operating systems.

The following are the functions in the pthread.h library that create, manipulate, and exit the threads.

- pthread_create
- pthread_join
- pthread_self
- pthread_equal
- pthread_exit
- pthread_cancel
- pthread_detach

pthread_create

pthread_create creates a new thread with a thread descriptor. A descriptor is an information container of the thread state, execution status, the process that it belongs to, related threads, stack reference information, and thread-specific resource information allocated by the process. This function takes four arguments as parameters. The return type of this function is an integer.

The following shows the syntax.

```
int pthread_create(pthread_t *thread,
            const pthread_attr_t *attr,
            void * (*start_routine)(void *),
            void *arg);
```

The following describes the parameters.

- pthread_t is a thread descriptor variable that takes the thread descriptor, has an argument, and returns the thread ID, which is an unsigned long integer.

- pthread_attr_t is an argument that determines all the properties assigned to a thread. If it is a normal default thread, then you set the attribute value to NULL; otherwise, the argument is changed based on the programmer's requirements.

- start_routine is an argument that points to the subroutines that execute by thread. The return type for this parameter is an void type because it typecasts return types explicitly. This argument takes a single value as a parameter. If you want to pass multiple arguments, a heterogeneous datatype should be passed that might be a struct.

- args is a parameter that depends on the previous parameter; it takes multiple parameters as an argument.

pthread_join

This function waits for the termination of another thread. It takes two parameters as arguments and returns the integer type. It returns 0 on successful termination and –1 if any failure occurs.

The following shows the syntax.

```
int pthread_join(pthread_t, *thread,
                void **thread_return)
```

The following describes the parameters.

- thread takes the ID of the thread that is currently waiting for termination

- thread_return is an argument that points to the exit status of the termination thread, which is a NULL value.

pthread_self

This function returns the thread ID of the currently running thread. The return type of this thread is an integer or the thread_t descriptor. It takes zero parameters as arguments.

The following shows the syntax.

```
pthread_t pthread_self()
```

or

```
int pthread_self()
```

pthread_equal

This function checks whether two threads are equal or not. If the two threads are equal, then the function returns a nonzero value. If the threads are not equal, then it is zero. It takes two parameters as arguments and returns the integer as output.

The following shows the syntax.

```
int pthread_equal(pthread_t thread1,
                  pthread_t thread2);
```

The following describes the parameters.

thread1 and thread2 are the IDs for the first and second thread, respectively.

pthread_exit

This function terminates a calling thread. It takes one argument as a parameter and returns nothing.

The following shows the syntax.

```
void pthread_exit(void *retval);
```

The following describes the parameters.

retval is the return value of a thread that you want to detach it.

pthread_cancel

This function is used for thread cancellation. It takes one parameter as an argument and returns an integer value.

The following shows the syntax.

```
int pthread_cancel(pthread_t thread);
```

The following describes the parameter.

pthread is the thread ID of the thread that you want to cancel.

pthread_detach

This function detaches a thread in a detached state. It takes a thread descriptor as an argument and returns the integer value as output.

The following shows the syntax.

```
int pthread_detach(pthread_t thread);
```

The following describes the parameter.

thread is a descriptor variable that is passed as an ID, which you want to detach it.

These functions are the most common functions in multithreading operations.

Creating Threads

As discussed earlier, the pthread_create function creates threads. This section deals with thread creation and how to execute multithreaded programs. It examines the weird behavior of multithreaded programs and how to overcome ambiguous output during the development process. A simple multithreaded program can be created in simple three steps.

1. Import the required libraries. Our program includes the headers that are necessary for the operation.

    ```
    #include<stdio.h>    // Standard I/O Routines Library
    #include<unistd.h>   // Unix Standard Library
    #include<pthread.h>  // POSIX Thread Creation Library
    ```

CHAPTER 2   MULTITHREADING IN C

2. Develop the thread function to make it multithreaded. The thread function must have a return type as a pointer.

```
void *customThreadFunction(){

    for(int i = 0; i < 15; i++){
        printf("I am a Custom Thread Function Created By
        Programmer.\n");
        sleep(1);
    }

    return NULL;
}
```

In this custom thread function, a for loop is written, which iterates 15 times [0–14] and prints the statement using the printf function. It sleeps for one second after the iteration of every print statement. sleep() is available in the unistd.h library.

3. In this step, the main function comes into the picture. In the main function, you need to create a thread descriptor variable and method. The following program tells you whether a thread is created successfully or not. The pthread_create function returns the status codes 0 and 1 for success or failure. If the thread is successful, the thread function executes; otherwise, you exit out of the program.

In the pthread_create function, the first argument is the address of the thread descriptor variable. Since this deals with the custom default threads, don't bother with the second argument; take it as a NULL value. The third value is a custom thread function that is executed in the thread. The last argument is also NULL because, in this custom thread function, there aren't any arguments to pass.

```
int main(){

    pthread_t thread;    // Thread Descriptor
```

```
    int status;          // Status Variable to store the Status of the
                            thread.

    status = pthread_create(&thread, NULL, customThreadFunction, NULL);

    /*  status = 0 ==> If thread is created Sucessfully.
        status = 1 ==> If thread is unable to create.    */

    if(!status){
        printf("Custom Created Successfully.\n");
    }else{
        printf("Unable to create the Custom Thread.\n");
        return 0;
    }

    // Main Function For loop
    for(int i = 0; i < 15; i++){
        printf("I am the process thread created by compiler By
        default.\n");
        sleep(1);
    }

    return 0;
}
```

After the compilation is done, run the `./a.out` command, which gives the output for your program.

```
> gcc thread_creation.c
> ./a.out
Custom Created Successfully.
I am the process thread created by compiler By default.
I am a Custom Thread Function Created By Programmer.
I am the process thread created by compiler By default.
I am a Custom Thread Function Created By Programmer.
I am the process thread created by compiler By default.
I am a Custom Thread Function Created By Programmer.
I am the process thread created by compiler By default.
I am a Custom Thread Function Created By Programmer.
I am a Custom Thread Function Created By Programmer.
I am the process thread created by compiler By default.
I am a Custom Thread Function Created By Programmer.
I am the process thread created by compiler By default.
I am a Custom Thread Function Created By Programmer.
I am the process thread created by compiler By default.
I am a Custom Thread Function Created By Programmer.
I am the process thread created by compiler By default.
I am a Custom Thread Function Created By Programmer.
I am the process thread created by compiler By default.
I am the process thread created by compiler By default.
I am a Custom Thread Function Created By Programmer.
I am a Custom Thread Function Created By Programmer.
I am the process thread created by compiler By default.
I am a Custom Thread Function Created By Programmer.
I am the process thread created by compiler By default.
I am a Custom Thread Function Created By Programmer.
I am the process thread created by compiler By default.
I am a Custom Thread Function Created By Programmer.
I am the process thread created by compiler By default.
I am a Custom Thread Function Created By Programmer.
I am the process thread created by compiler By default.
```

Figure 2-9. *The output of the thread creation program*

The output of my program may differ from yours. This is the ambiguity that is hidden inside multithreaded programs.

Next, let's learn how to overcome this ambiguity by using different functions in our program.

Practical Examples of Multithreading
Thread Termination

Termination of a thread is mandatory in certain situations. In our program, let's terminate the thread after the three iterations. It is done using the pthread_exit function, which takes a single argument. Let's pass that argument as NULL since this deals with the default threads. You can see the difference in the thread termination in the output.

```c
#include<stdio.h>    // Standard I/O Routines Library
#include<unistd.h>   // Unix Standard Library
#include<pthread.h>  // POSIX Thread Creation Library

void *customThreadFunction(){

    for(int i = 0; i < 5; i++){
        printf("I am a Custom Thread Function Created By Programmer.\n");
        sleep(1);
        if(i == 3){
            printf("My JOB is Done. I am now being terminated by
            programmer.\n");
            pthread_exit(NULL);
        }
    }

    return NULL;
}

int main(){

    pthread_t thread;    // Thread Descriptor
    pthread_create(&thread, NULL, customThreadFunction, NULL);

    for(int i = 0; i < 5; i++){
        printf("I am the process thread created by compiler By default.\n");
        sleep(1);
    }

    return 0;
}
```

The output of the program is shown in Figure 2-10.

```
> gcc thread_termination.c
> ./a.out
I am the process thread created by compiler By default.
I am a Custom Thread Function Created By Programmer.
I am the process thread created by compiler By default.
I am a Custom Thread Function Created By Programmer.
I am the process thread created by compiler By default.
I am a Custom Thread Function Created By Programmer.
I am the process thread created by compiler By default.
I am a Custom Thread Function Created By Programmer.
I am the process thread created by compiler By default.
My JOB is Done. I am now being terminated by programmer.
```

Figure 2-10. *The output of the thread termination program*

Thread Equal Property

If you want to check whether two threads are equal or not, use the thread_equal function, which checks the equality condition.

```c
#include<stdio.h>    // Standard I/O Routines Library
#include<unistd.h>   // Unix Standard Library
#include<pthread.h> // POSIX Thread Creation Library

void *customThreadFunction(){
    printf("This is my custom thread\n");
    return NULL;
}

int main(){

    pthread_t thread1, thread2;
    pthread_create(&thread1, NULL, customThreadFunction, NULL);
    pthread_create(&thread2, NULL, customThreadFunction, NULL);

    if(pthread_equal(thread1, thread2)){
        printf("Two threads are Equal..!\n");
    }else{
        printf("Two threads are not equal\n");
```

```
        }
    return 0;
}
```

The output is shown in Figure 2-11.

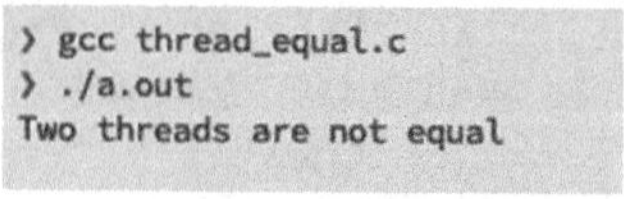

```
> gcc thread_equal.c
> ./a.out
Two threads are not equal
```

Figure 2-11. *The output of the thread equal program*

Passing a Single Argument to a Thread Function

Passing arguments to the thread function is done with a few changes to the pthread_ create function arguments, as shown in the following code.

```c
#include <stdio.h>
#include <pthread.h>

void *sayGreetings(void *input) {
    printf("Hello %s\n", (char *)input);
    pthread_exit(NULL);
}

int main() {

    char name[50];
    printf("Enter your name: \n");
    fgets(name,50, stdin);

    pthread_t thread;
    pthread_create(&thread, NULL, sayGreetings, name);
    pthread_join(thread, NULL);
    return 0;
}
```

The pthread_create function takes four arguments as parameters. In general, if a custom thread does not take any arguments, then you should pass fourth parameter as a NULL value. If your custom thread function requires a single parameter as an argument, then you pass that variable to the fourth variable. Passing multiple arguments is discussed in the next example.

Figure 2-12 shows the output.

```
> gcc thread_argument.c
> ./a.out
Enter your name:
Abhi
Hello Abhi
```

Figure 2-12. *Thread argument program output*

Passing Multiple Arguments as Parameters

If you want to pass multiple arguments for a custom thread function, then you use heterogeneous data types (i.e., structures that collect all your required data into one variable, which pass as a fourth argument in the pthread_create function).

```c
#include <stdio.h>
#include<stdlib.h>
#include <pthread.h>

// Data Collector.
struct arguments {
    char* name;
    int age;
    char *bloodGroup;
};

// Thread Function
void *sayGreetings(void *data) {
    printf("Name: %s", ((struct arguments*)data)->name);
    printf("Age: %d\n", ((struct arguments*)data)->age);
    printf("Blood Group: %s\n", ((struct arguments*)data)->bloodGroup);
    return NULL;
}
```

```
int main() {

    struct arguments *person = (struct arguments *)malloc(sizeof(struct
    arguments));
    printf("This is a Simple Data Collection Application\n");
    char bloodGroup[5], name[50];
    int age;
    printf("Enter the name of the person: ");
    fgets(name, 50, stdin);
    printf("Enter the age of the person: ");
    scanf("%d",&age);
    printf("Enter the person's Blood Group: ");
    scanf("%s", bloodGroup);

    person->name = name;
    person->age = age;
    person->bloodGroup = bloodGroup;

    pthread_t thread;
    pthread_create(&thread, NULL, sayGreetings, (void *)person);
    pthread_join(thread, NULL);
    return 0;
}
```

This example creates a pointer that points to a struct, which is cast to a void pointer as (void *) and passes to the pthread_thread function.

Figure 2-13 shows the output.

```
⟩ gcc thread_multiple_arguments.c
⟩ ./a.out
This is a Simple Data Collection Application
Enter the name of the person: Santhosh
Enter the age of the person: 17
Enter the person's Blood Group: B-ve
Name: Santhosh
Age: 17
Blood Group: B-ve
```

Figure 2-13. *Thread multiple argument output*

The Relationship Between Threads and the CPU

Table 2-2 defines the relationship between threads and the CPU.

Table 2-2. *Relationship Between Thread and CPU*

Parameters	Thread	CPU
Definition	A thread is a small segment in a process. It is a virtual component that manages tasks in an operating system.	The CPU is a hardware component that contains multiple cores. A core is a single computing component that helps the CPU execute and read program instructions. The number of cores is directly proportional to the processing speed.
Work	The process assigns a thread's work.	The tasks are assigned by the threads to process.
Task	The task of the threads is to achieve concurrency.	The task of the CPU is to multitask and multiprogram.
Dependent	It is dependent on the CPU.	It is dependent on the core (i.e., internal component).
Processing Units	It requires multiple processing units.	It requires a single processing unit.
Benefits	Threads improve the throughput and computation speed.	It performs arithmetical and logical operations in a system.
Example	Running a visual code editor application is a multithreaded-based process	Running multiple applications, like a browser, code editor, and iTunes, at the same time.

Multithreading Use Cases

There are a lot of practical use cases that implement multithreading. All the topics in this chapter used socket programming, which is discussed in Chapter 8. But briefly, in socket programming, multithreading is helpful for listening to requests from various clients. This section looks at things that use multithreading. Here are some of the applications that use it.

- Web crawler applications

- Online booking applications, which runs on PHP or Java

- 3D games

- Integrated development environments

- Video editing software

- Text editors

- Word processors

And the list goes on, but here are a few types of applications that internally use multithreading. There are certain issues that programmers face during the usage of multithreading, but handling these issues is done with synchronization. All these topics are covered in the upcoming chapters.

Summary

In this chapter, you were introduced to threads on an operating system. The chapter also discussed the following.

- The life cycle of a process and thread

- The importance of multithreading and its support in C

- Creating a thread in C and examples in the pthread.h library

- The differences between a CPU and threads

- Multithreading use cases

CHAPTER 3

Introduction to POSIX Standards and System-Level APIs

POSIX standards help maintain compatibility between operating systems. System-level APIs help to efficiently develop applications very within a short development period. In this chapter, you learn about the following introductory topics.

- The POSIX standard

- POSIX support

- Introduction to APIs

- Importance of APIs

- Built-in C Standard APIs

Understanding POSIX Standards

POSIX is the acronym for *Portable Operating System Interface* on Unix-based operating systems. They are IEEE standards to formalize certain common standards in all operating systems in the enterprise market.

© Sri Manikanta Palakollu 2021
S. M. Palakollu, *Practical System Programming with C*, https://doi.org/10.1007/978-1-4842-6321-1_3

In the olden days, programmers struggled to develop an application for computer systems. Before POSIX standards, there were no common standards for developing a computer operating system model, so developers needed to develop their applications for every model—from scratch—to be compatible with all systems. This increased development time and the cost of an application. Debugging was also very difficult because of new bugs and issues in every new computer model, which caused a lot of problems for developers.

To avoid these issues, IEEE introduced standard rules to practice when developing new computer models. These standards helped develop all kinds of applications. Developers no longer need to develop new code for new system models. These standard rules are classified into four main categories.

- POSIX.1

- POSIX.1b

- POSIX.1c

- POSIX.2

POSIX.1 Standards

POSIX.1 standards deal with the core services of all operating system models. The following are features included in this standard.

- Process creation and control

- Process triggers

- Files and directory operations

- Segmentation faults

- Memory faults

- Floating-point exceptions

- Pipes

- Signals

- Standard C library implementation

- Standard I/O interface and control

These are some of the core features that the IEEE addressed to improve the interface of all operating systems.

POSIX.1b Standards

Along with the POSIX.1 standards, there are additional core features specifically related to real-time application development. These POSIX.1b rules include the following topics.

- CPU scheduling algorithms
- Message passing
- Shared memory
- Semaphore
- Memory-locking interfaces
- Synchronous and asynchronous data transfer interfaces

All the core features are covered in upcoming chapters.

POSIX.1c Standards

This standard category includes core features related to multithreading.

- Thread creation
- Thread control
- Thread deletion
- Thread synchronization
- Thread scheduling

POSIX.2 Standards

POSIX.2 standards address the core functionality features of an operating system.

- uname
- tty
- cd
- ls

- mkdir

- echo

- cp

- rm

- mv

This standard list includes all common utilities and the tools that are commonly used by the users.

POSIX Support

All OS models do not use POSIX standards. macOS uses the complete POSIX standards for its operating system, but most Linux distros use the Linux Standard Base (LSB), which includes more powerful features than POSIX. It is a superset of POSIX standards but also independent of POSIX standards. The Windows 10 operating system uses POSIX as a subsystem with the same standard features.

Introduction to APIs

API stands for *application programming interface*. It is a collection of protocols and subroutines that communicate between various systems and subsystems. APIs make developers' lives a lot easier. There are several types of APIs.

- Public API or open API

- Private API

- Partner API

- Composite API

All the APIs are normal web services standard APIs, but this book concentrates on system-level APIs. System-level APIs are normal programs written by developers to improve the core functionality of a programming language. A system-level API has two different modes: user mode and supervisor mode (see Figure 3-1).

User Mode

In user mode, developers typically develop programs to incorporate or manipulate custom activities in the system. The activities performed at the user level is done with the help of System-level API. The activities include file creation, directory creation, and similar basic activities.

Supervisor Mode

In supervisor mode, system calls perform the actions written by the developers. These built-in functions and libraries are very helpful when it comes to performing system-level tasks. The system call in supervisor mode executes the calls that are made from the user mode. Programs are written to perform some action(s).

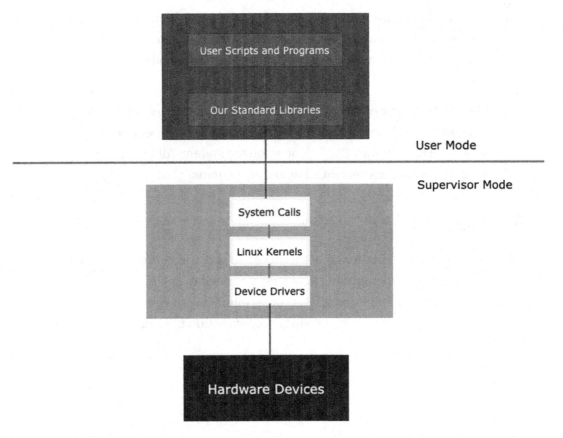

Figure 3-1. *Working API*

The Importance of System-Level APIs

Built-in system APIs improve the performance of the developed system. There is no need to write the code from scratch. Built-in functions and libraries are not required to perform testing because there are tested rigorously before release. The following are some of the benefits of using these functions.

- **Performance**: These libraries are under active development, and developers continuously try to improve the performance of existing functions. Also, they use standard algorithms, such as standard sorting and searching algorithms, to get the best performance.

- **Reliable code**: There are fewer errors because most of the activities are done with built-in functions, and because the libraries are under active development.

- **Reduces development time**: Most of the code is written by developers to perform a particular activity, which reduces development time because there is no need to write code from scratch.

- **System-independent**: C-program compiled binaries are system-dependent, but these built-in libraries are system-independent, which means that they don't depend on the system. All the built-in functions work the same on all operating systems.

Built-in APIs in C

Standard libraries are used in the rest of this book. To perform certain system core activities with a specific programming language, you need to check whether the language has a standard library that allows you to interact with your OS or not. Luckily, the C language provides support for a system's core functionality. Table 3-1 lists the most commonly used libraries.

Table 3-1. *Most Common Libraries*

Library	Functionality
\<stdio.h\>	This library contains all the standard input and output operation functions: 10 macros and 41 functions. The most popular functions are printf and scanf.
\<stdlib.h\>	This is a standard library in C that is mainly used for general-purpose programming. It contains the memory allocation and deallocation functions that perform dynamic activities.
\<unistd.h\>	This library provides the standard interface for the POSIX API.
\<sys/types.h\>	This library contains standard derived data types, which are helpful in system-level programming.
\<signal.h\>	This library handles the signal activities in an operating system.
\<time.h\>	This library provides support for time and date activities in a standard manner.
\<sys/stat.h\>	This library determines the file system status and activity.
\<fcntl.h\>	This library is a part of the POSIX API that manipulates files, such as changing permissions.
\<sys/ipc.h\>	This library deals with three major core tasks that include interprocess communication activity (i.e., message queues, semaphores, and shared memory).
\<sys/msg.h\>	This library works with the \<sys/ipc.h\> library to deal with IPC activity.
\<semaphore.h\>	This library performs the semaphore activity in an operating system. It is also a part of the POSIX library.
\<sys/shm.h\>	This library performs shared memory activities.
\<sys/wait.h\>	This library places a process into a waiting state.
\<stdargs.h\>	This library handles the variable argument activity that takes input directly from the command-line.

Summary

This chapter discussed topics related to the POSIX environment and the various C built-in libraries. You were also introduced to system-level APIs.

CHAPTER 4

Files and Directories

You have learned about command-line topics in Linux. You were introduced to multithreading and the practical implementation of multithreading in C. You saw API support in C to develop efficient applications. This chapter discusses files and directories. By the end of this chapter, you should have a deep knowledge of the core concepts regarding Linux files, directories, and storage mechanisms. The chapter's code examples and discussions cover the following topics.

- File system

- Inodes and file metadata

- Inode storage mechanisms

- System calls and I/O operations for files

- Systems calls for file permissions

- File permission checks

- Soft links

- Hard links

- System calls for directories

File Systems

Storage is one of the most essential components of an OS. The storage system must have a well-organized structure, and it must be easy to access the content. In Linux/Unix-based systems, everything is a file, which maintains the consistency that makes the files easy to access. The file system in Unix is groups files into folders based on purpose and use in a well-organized way. For most beginners, this seems intimidating. But once you understand the purpose of each directory that is part of the Unix file system, then it becomes easy to use and work with it.

© Sri Manikanta Palakollu 2021
S. M. Palakollu, *Practical System Programming with C*, https://doi.org/10.1007/978-1-4842-6321-1_4

The Unix file system looks like a tree structure. It consists of several directories, and each directory consists of several specific files and subdirectories. In Unix, all the directories are in the root directory (/). The entire Unix file system structure is represented in Figure 4-1.

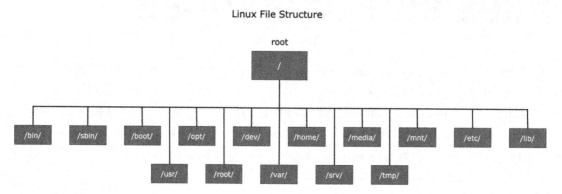

Figure 4-1. *Linux file structure*

- **/ (the root directory)**

  - This directory is called the *root directory*.

  - All the files and directories in your Linux or Unix system are grouped into this root directory.

  - In this directory, only root users have permission to write.

- **/bin (binaries)**

  - This directory contains all the essential binaries in the operating system.

  - The most frequently used Linux commands in a single-user mode are located in this directory.

  - Examples of available commands are cd, mkdir, ls, mv, and cp.

  - Shells like bash, ksh, csh, zsh are located in this directory only. (i.e., (/bin/bash, /bin/sh, etc.).

- **/sbin (system binaries)**

  - This directory is similar to the /bin directory, but it contains the system administration binaries, which are executed by the root user.

- The commands and programs available in this directory are only executed by the superuser.

- The most common programs available in /sbin are ifconfig, iptables, and reboot.

- **/boot (boot files)**

  - This directory contains all boot loader–related files, which are very important for booting an operating system.

  - All the files in this directory are static boot files. This directory does not contain any boot configuration files.

  - An example of a boot loader file is a GRUB loader file, which boots an operating system when you power-on your laptop or desktop.

- **/opt (optional packages)**

  - This directory consists of all the files that are not part of the default installation.

  - Third-party software installed on your system that did not come as a default installation on Unix/Linux. Proprietary software installation files are placed in this directory.

  - Examples of software installed on Unix/Linux from third-party sources include Apache server and Apache Tomcat server.

- **/dev (device files)**

  - The files in this directory represent the hardware device files.

  - As with everything in Linux, devices are represented by a directory or a file; so, all device-supported files for the system are placed here.

  - This directory consists of special device files that come with the installation of the operating system. They help the operating system to support all types of devices detected while running the operating system.

- **/home (home directory)**

  - This is the home directory, which contains each user's files.

  - This directory consists of the user's personal data and configuration files. The configuration files in this directory vary from user to user.

  - If your system user name is Alex, then you have a home folder located at /home/Alex. The number of user accounts on your system equals the number of subdirectories present.

- **/media (removable media)**

  - This directory consists of all the removable device directories.

  - When an external removable device is mounted in a Linux system, then automatically, a new directory is created under this directory.

  - When a USB is inserted to a laptop/PC that is running on a Linux/Unix-based operating system, then the /media directory creates a directory for the removable USB. This directory contains all the removable media files that are automatically created by the operating system.

- **/mnt (mount directory)**

  - This directory consists of all the mounted files in a system.

  - Suppose that your PC is dual booted (*dual boot* means you can have two operating systems on one PC). The number is not restricted. You can have any number, but hard disk space is limited. In a dual boot PC, all the other operating system mounted files are placed in this directory.

  - System administrators use this directory to unmount a mounted file system. Normal users can't mount a filesystem without root privileges.

- **/etc (configuration files)**

  - This directory consists of all the configuration files that are used by all the programs in a Linux operating system.

- System-level configuration files are placed in this directory. The user-level configuration files are placed in the user-level home directory.

- Startup and shutdown scripts are located in this directory.

- You can configure it with editors for your own use; for instance, the configuration of a LAMP server.

- **/lib (system libraries)**

  - This directory contains the essential libraries needed by the binaries that are in the /bin and /sbin directories.

- **/usr (user programs and data)**

  - This directory contains all the binary files and applications that are used by the user.

  - /usr/lib contains the binaries for /bin and /sbin.

  - Applications installed from the source are placed in the /usr/local directory.

  - /usr/sbin contains the binary files for system administrators. If you are unable to find the required files in this directory, go to the root level /sbin directory.

  - This directory contains the source code for second-level programs, which do not come from the default installation.

  - All the files in this folder have read-only access because they are system-related binary files.

- **/root (root home directory)**

  - This is the home directory for the root user; it is not a system root directory.

  - Most people confuse / and /root. The major difference is that / is a system-level root directory. And /root is the user-level root directory.

- **/var (variable data files)**

    - This directory consists of all the user data files in a system. This data refers to the system data.

    - This directory contains log files under /var/log; packages and database files under /var/lib; and temporary files under /var/tmp.

- **/srv (service data files)**

    All the internal operating system service data files are located in this directory; for instance, files that are related to local servers are found under this directory.

- **/tmp (temporary files)**

    - All the temporary files created by the system or user are placed in this directory. If the user has root privileges, then he/she can put the temporary files in any location, but /tmp is the recommended and system-assigned one.

    - All the system-level temporary files are stored in this directory.

    - The files in this directory are deleted when the system is rebooted. The deletion of temporary files is dependent on the Linux distribution, however, because some Linux distros do not delete the temporary files in the system after every reboot.

    - Users can manually delete the files in the tmp directory.

It seems a bit hard to remember everything, but once you start using these directories, it becomes easier. Each directory stores specific programs and utility applications. Unlike Windows, Unix-based systems don't have drive letters, like C: drive and D: drive. You can create partitions in Linux, but all the partitioned disk space is packed into a tree-like structure that has a root (/) directory.

File Metadata and Inodes

Everything is a file descriptor in Linux. A *file descriptor* is a number that uniquely identifies a file that is open on an operating system. The file descriptor contains information about the opened file. Every file has certain key attributes to identify its properties. Regular files include images, audio, video, and other raw files that usually have metadata associated with them. All the file attributes are stores in an inode.

An *inode* is a data structure that tracks all the information about a file. An inode plays a very crucial role in Unix-based operating systems. When a user wants to access a file, the operating system first searches for the inode number in an associated inode table. The storage of inode numbers in an operating system and finding a particular file using the path is explained in Figure 4-3. Every inode has a unique number. An inode number is the index number that is associated with each inode. OS searches for an inode number come from an inode table. The Unix storage system is a bit different from the Windows storage system, but it is more efficient. The structure of an inode is represented in Figure 4-2.

Structure of Inode

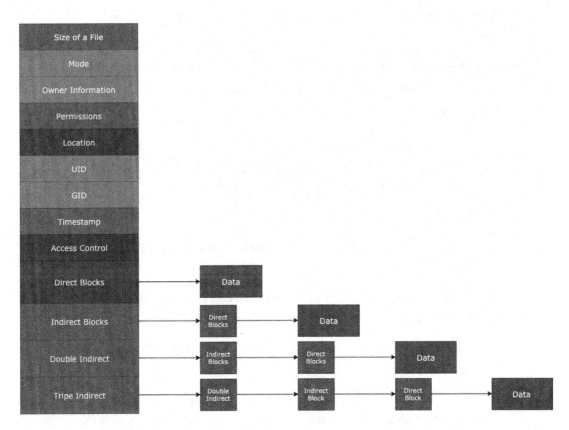

Figure 4-2. *Inode structure*

- **Size** stores the file size.
- **Mode** stores information on the file's permissions and the type (i.e., directory, file, device directory, etc.).

- **Owner information** points to the person who created the file.

- **Permissions** contain all the permissions levels for a file (i.e., user, group, other users).

- **Location** describes the exact location of the file on the operating system.

- **UID** is short for *user ID*. It stores the user ID of the currently working user and represents the owner of the file.

- **GID** stands for *group ID*. It stores the group ID of the file that belongs to and represents the group owner.

- **Timestamp** stores the inode creation time and when the file was modified.

- **Access control** contains information on the special privileges given to groups and other users (the outside real-world users).

- **Direct block**

  - Linux usually follows the file system ext2, et3, et4; but for now, we discuss the ext2 file system, which is popular. In the ext2 file system, an inode consists of 12 direct block pointers.

  - The first 12 block pointers are direct.

  - The direct block directly points to the file data, as shown in Figure 4-2.

  - In the direct block system, 12 blocks are reserved for storing the file pointer's address and directly pointing to the data/file.

  - Each direct block points to a file that is 4 KB. In total, direct blocks can store 48 KB.

  - Direct block storage is very limited (i.e., 48 KB). It can't point to large data files or directories. Indirect blocks overcome this issue.

- **Indirect block**

  - It points to the files or directories that are greater than 4 KB and less than or equal to 4 MB.

- It is more advanced than the direct block method. It creates 1024 different blocks internally. Each block stores 4 KB of data, which is very small. Data pointers point to the 1024 blocks. Since each block stores 4 KB of data, this results in a total 4 MB of data. This is called the *indirect block mechanism.*

- The Unix/Linux system is intelligent at detecting and effectively monitoring data. If the size of a file/directory is more than 4 MB, it automatically moves to the double indirect block method.

- Data pointers internally point to the 1024 block pointers that store the file data.

- **Double indirect block**

  - It creates 1024 different blocks to point the data. Each block can store 4 MB of data. Internally, it points to the indirect block address, which can point up to 4 MB.

  - It can point up to 4 GB of data. If the file or directory is greater than 4 GB, it automatically transfers the pointer data to the triple indirect block.

  - It internally points to 1024 indirect block pointers.

- **Triple indirect block**

  - It creates 1024 different blocks to point the data. Each block can store 4 GB of data. Internally, it points to the double indirect block address, which can point up to 4 GB.

  - It can point to as much as 4 TB of data. It internally points to the 1024 double indirect block pointers.

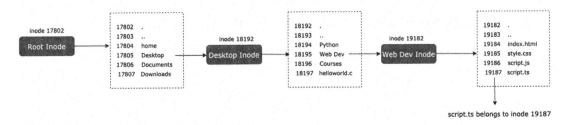

Figure 4-3. Structure of inode for file storage mechanism in Linux

Figure 4-3 shows an inode pointing mechanism structure that represents accessing a file named script.ts on the operating system. Suppose that a user wants to access a file on the operating system at /root/Desktop/WebDev/script.ts.

Initially, the root directory has a specific inode number that points to the root number. It consists of several files and folders. In our situation, the root directory has home, desktop, documents, and downloads directories. The desktop directory has an inode number that consists of several lists of files and folders (i.e., Python, Web Dev, Courses directories, and a helloworld.c program file).

Each directory and program file has its own inode number. When I navigate to the Web Dev directory, it has a separate inode number that points to another set of files and directories (that include index.html, style.css, script.js, script.ts), which have different inode numbers. The searched file is available in the Web Dev directory. If the given file name is not available in the specified location, an error is immediately thrown. All the inode numbers are internally connected to provide better and faster access to files and directories.

When you enter a directory and input the ls command in the command line, all the files and directories in that directory are displayed based on the inode number. This happens because of all the inode numbers of files and directories in that directory point to an array of inode numbers that point to the parent directory. This is represented in Figure 4-3; for example, the desktop inode is pointing to six different inode numbers. Those are the files and directories in the desktop directory.

System Calls and I/O Operations for Files

The most common operations that you can perform on files are read, write, delete, and modify the content. This section explains dealing with file manipulation programmatically. Our program uses core system calls to manipulate the tasks. To get more information on a system call, you can use the man command. For example, man creat gives complete information on the creat system call (see Figure 4-4).

```
CREAT(2)                    BSD System Calls Manual                 CREAT(2)

NAME
     creat -- create a new file

LIBRARY
     Standard C Library (libc, -lc)

SYNOPSIS
     #include <fcntl.h>

     int
     creat(const char *path, mode_t mode);

DESCRIPTION
     This interface is made obsolete by: open(2).

     The creat() function is the same as:

           open(path, O_CREAT | O_TRUNC | O_WRONLY, mode);

SEE ALSO
     open(2)

HISTORY
     The creat() function appeared in Version 6 AT&T UNIX.

BSD                          June 2, 1993                      BSD
(END)
```

Figure 4-4. *Man command information on creat system call*

These system calls set an error number if they fail to perform the operation. The error numbers analyze why the system call is unable to perform a particular activity and may quickly debug the application.

To get the error code for your application, you need to use the error function explicitly to print the message to the console. Table 4-1 describes some of the most useful error codes.

Table 4-1. *Useful Error Codes*

Error Number	Error Code	Description
1	EPERM	Operation Not Permitted
2	ENOENT	No Such File Or Directory
3	ESRCH	No Such Process
4	EINTR	System Call Interrupted
5	EIO	I/O Error
6	ENXIO	No such device or address

(continued)

Table 4-1. (*continued*)

Error Number	Error Code	Description
8	ENOEXEC	Exec Format Error
9	EBADF	Bad File Number
10	ECHILD	No child processes available
11	EAGAIN	Try again
12	ENOMEM	Out of Memory
13	EACCES	Permission Denied
14	EFAULT	Bad Address
16	EBUSY	Device or Resource Busy
17	EEXIST	File Exist
20	ENOTDIR	Not a Directory
21	EISDIR	Is a Directory
22	EINVAL	Invalid Argument
23	ENFILE	File Table Overflow
24	EMFILE	Too many open files
27	EFBIG	File too large
28	ENOSPACE	No Space Available on device
29	ESPIPE	Illegal Seek
30	EROFS	Read-Only File System
32	EPIPE	Broken Pipe
33	EDOM	Math argument out of the domain
34	ERANGE	Math results not representable
39	ENOTEMPTY	Directory Not Empty
40	ELOOP	Too many symbolic links occurred
62	ETIME	Timer Expired
64	ENONET	The machine is not available in the network

(*continued*)

Table 4-1. (*continued*)

Error Number	Error Code	Description
65	ENOPKG	Package is not available
71	EPROTO	Protocol Error
86	ESTRPIPE	Stream Pipe Error
87	EUSERS	Too many users
91	EPROTOTYPE	Protocol error for socket

The following are the system calls that are available for file operations.

- creat

- open

- close

- read

- write

creat

This system call creates a new empty file with a system call. It is available in the fcntl.h library, which is a file handling library for Unix and Linux. The return type for this function is an integer. If file creation is successful, it returns a non-negative integer. If the creation of the file fails, it returns –1.

The following shows the syntax.

int creat(char *filename, mode_t mode);

- The first parameter in the creat function is the name of a file.

- The second parameter, mode, deals with the permissions of the file. The permission modes are different from normal Linux file system permissions. There are various modes available for this flag, but the following are the most common modes.

    - O_RDONLY: If you set this flag mode to the creat function, the file has read-only permission.

- O_WRONLY: This mode gives write permissions.

- O_RDWR: This mode gives both read and write permissions.

- O_EXCL: This flag mode prevents the creation of a file if it already exists.

- O_APPEND: This mode appends the content to existing file data without overriding it.

- O_CREAT: This flag mode creates a file if it does not exist.

If you want to use multiple modes at the same time, you can use the bitwise OR operator.

Here's an example.

```
#include<stdio.h>
#include<fcntl.h>
int main(){

    int file_descriptor;
    char filename[255];

    printf("Enter the filename: ");
    scanf("%s", filename);
    // Setting Permission to Read and Write Access for the file.
    file_descriptor = creat(filename, O_RDWR | O_CREAT);
    if(file_descriptor != -1){
        printf("File Created Successfully!");
    }else{
        printf("Unable to Create the File.");
    }

    return 0;
}
```

A file descriptor is an integer value that identifies the open file in a process. This program creates a new file with the given permissions set.

open

The open system call function opens a file and can perform read and write operations based on the mode set to the function. An open system call can also create a file. If the specified filename is not available, then it automatically creates a new file with the given name. The return type of this function is an integer. If the file opens successfully, it returns a positive integer value; otherwise, it returns –1.

The following shows the syntax.

int open(const char *filepath, int flags, ...);

- The first parameter deals with the absolute path of a file that you want to open.

- The flags that are passed as a second argument are O_RDONLY, O_WRONLY, O_RDWR, and so forth.

Here's an example.

```
#include<stdio.h>
#include<fcntl.h>

int main(){

    int file_descriptor;
    char filename[255];

    printf("Enter the filename: ");
    scanf("%s", filename);
    // Setting Permission to Read Only for the file.
    file_descriptor = open(filename, O_RDONLY);
    /*
    On Success: It returns any value other than -1.

    */

    if(file_descriptor != -1){
        printf("%s Opened Successfully!",filename);
    }else{
```

```
        printf("Unable to Open %s",filename);
    }

    return 0;
}
```

This program prints a statement on whether the given file is open or not.

close

This system call closes the file descriptor that was created to open, create, or read the contents in a file. The return type of this function is an integer. If the file descriptor is closed successfully, it returns 0; otherwise, it returns –1.

The following shows the syntax.

```
int close(int file_descriptor);
```

file_descriptor is an integer value that identifies the open file in a process.
Here's an example.

```
#include<stdio.h>
#include<fcntl.h>

int close(int file_descriptor);

int main(){

    int file_descriptor;
    char filename[255];

    printf("Enter the filename: ");
    scanf("%s", filename);
    // Setting Permission to Read Write for the file.
    file_descriptor = open(filename, O_RDWR, 0);

    if(file_descriptor != -1){
        printf("File Opened Successfully!\n");
    }else{
        printf("Unable to Open the File.\n");
    }
```

```c
int close_status = close(file_descriptor);
// Checks the condition and prints the appropriate statement.
/*
 Success: 0
 Error: -1
 */
if(close_status == 0){
    printf("File Descriptor is closed Successfully\n");
}else{
    printf("File Descriptor is not closed\n");
}

return 0;
}
```

This program opens a file and closes the file descriptor after the task is done. After the file descriptor is opened and work is done, it is a good programming practice to close the descriptor.

read

This function system call reads the content of a file that was indicated by a file descriptor. The return type of this function is an integer. It returns –1 if an error occurs or when any signal interrupt occurs during a read operation. A successful read of a file returns the number of bytes read during the operation.

The following shows the syntax.

```c
size_t read (int file_descriptor,
            void* buffer,
            size_t size);
```

- file_descriptor is a unique integer value that identifies the open file in a process.

- The **buffer** argument reads the file data.

- **size** is the third argument indicates the size of the buffer that you want to read from the file.

Here's an example.

```c
#include<stdio.h>
#include<stdlib.h>
#include<unistd.h>
#include <fcntl.h>

int main() {
  int file_descriptor, size;
 char filename[255];
 char *content = (char *) calloc(100, sizeof(char));

 printf("Enter the filename to read:");
 scanf("%[^\n]%*c",filename);

 file_descriptor = open(filename, O_RDONLY);
 // Program exit if the given file is not found.
 if (file_descriptor == -1) {
     perror("File Not found.");
     exit(1);
   }
 // read the Content from a given file descriptor.
 size = read(file_descriptor, content, 100);

 printf("Number of bytes returned are: %d\n", size);
 content[99] = '\0';
 printf("File Content: %s\n", content);

 // Closes the file descriptor.
 close(file_descriptor);

 return 0;
}
```

This program prints the number of bytes that were read and then prints the content.

write

This function writes content to a given file descriptor. The return type of this file is an integer. It returns –1 for an error or if any signal interrupt is raised; otherwise, it returns the number of bytes that are returned to a file.

The following shows the syntax.

```
size_t write (int file_descriptor,
              void* buffer,
              size_t size);
```

This function syntax is the same as the read function. But the key difference is that it writes the content to a file using the buffer. The read function reads the content from a file using a buffer.

Here's an example.

```
#include<stdio.h>
#include<unistd.h>
#include<stdlib.h>
#include<string.h>
#include <fcntl.h>

int main() {
  char filename[255];
 // Asking the Input from a User.
 printf("Enter the filename to open:\n");
 scanf("%[^\n]%*c", filename);
 int file_descriptor = open(filename, O_WRONLY | O_CREAT, 0777);

 if (file_descriptor == -1) {
    perror("File not Found.!");
    exit(1);
 }
 char content[1024];

 printf("Enter the content to write on a given file: ");
 // User Input to write into a File.
 scanf("%[^\n]%*c", content);
```

```
int size = write(file_descriptor, content, strlen(content));
printf("%d", size);
close(file_descriptor);

return 0;
}
```

This code opens a given file and asks the user to enter the content that they want to write to it. The write function writes content and prints the number of bytes written to a file.

Append Operations in Files Using System Calls

A write system call writes the content to the given file descriptor. But the O_RDWR flag mode overrides the content in an existing file. If you want to add more content to a file without overriding the existing content, the O_APPEND flag adds the new content at the end of the file without overriding any of the existing content.

Here's an example.

```
#include<stdio.h>
#include<unistd.h>
#include<stdlib.h>
#include<string.h>
#include <fcntl.h>

int main() {
  char filename[255];
 printf("Enter the filename to open:");
 scanf("%[^\n]%*c", filename);
 int file_descriptor = open(filename, O_WRONLY | O_CREAT | O_APPEND, 0777);
 if (file_descriptor == -1) {
    perror("File not Found.!");
    exit(1);
 }
 char content[1024];

 printf("Enter the content to write on a given file: ");
 scanf("%[^\n]%*c", content);
```

```
int size = write(file_descriptor, content, strlen(content));
 printf("%d %lu %d\n", file_descriptor, strlen(content), size);
 close(file_descriptor);

return 0;
}
```

This program appends content to an existing file without overwriting it.

File Permissions

In Chapter 1, you saw how to change the permissions of a file using the Linux commands. This section deals with changing file permissions programmatically and identifying all the permissions given to a particular file by using built-in attributes. These attributes are properties that check the permissions using R_OK, W_OK, F_OK, and X_OK.

chmod Function to Change Permissions

The chmod system call is available in the fcntl.h library. It changes the file permissions using the C program. The return type of this function is an integer. It returns 0 if it is successful and –1 if failure occurs.

The following shows the syntax.

int chmod(char *filepath, int mode);

- filepath is the first argument usually takes the complete file path with the respective file name as an argument.

- mode takes the new permission values as an argument. The value passed changes the file's permissions.

Here's an example.

```
#include<stdio.h>
#include<fcntl.h>
#include<stdlib.h>

int chmod(char *path, mode_t mode);

int main(){
```

93

```
    int permission_status;
    mode_ t new_permission_value;
    char filepath[100];

    // Taking the Input from the user
    printf("Enter the filename with path: ");
    scanf("%[^\n]%*c", filepath);
    printf("Enter the new permission set: ");
    // Permission Set value starts with 0.
    // Eg: if i want to set 444 to a particular file then i need to give
       like 0444.
    scanf("%d", &new_permission_value);

    // Setting the Permissions
    permission_status = chmod(filepath, new_permission_value);
    // 0 ---> On Success || -1 ---> On Failure.
    if (permission_status == 0){
        printf("New permissions are Setted Successfully.!");
    }else{
        printf("Permissions Changed Successfully");
    }

    return 0;
}
```

This program changes the permissions of a file. It returns a success statement if successful and returns a failure message if it is unable to change the permissions.

File Permissions Check

You can check a file's permissions with the access function in C, which is available in the unistd.h library. This return type of this function is an integer. It returns 0 if successful and –1 if failed.

The following shows the syntax.

```
int access(const char *filepath, int amode);
```

- `filepath` is the first argument that takes the complete file path (i.e., absolute path.

- The **amode** flag checks the permissions of a given file. The flags that pass for the second argument are any of the following.

  - R_OK: This flag tests the read permissions of a file.

  - W_OK: This flag tests the write permissions of a file.

  - F_OK: This flag tests whether a file exists or not.

  - X_OK: This flag tests the execute permissions of a file.

Now let's look at a simple example program that determines the read and write access permissions of a file.

```c
#include<stdio.h>
#include<unistd.h>

int main(){
    char filepath[100];
    // Taking the Input from the user
    printf("Enter the filename with path: ");
    scanf("%[^\n]%*c", filepath);

    int read_status, file_status, write_status;
    file_status = access(filepath, F_OK);
/*
    Returns
    -1 ----> If File Doesn't Exist
     0 ----> If File Exists
*/
    if(file_status == -1){
        printf("%s File does not exist in Location.\n", filepath);
        _exit(0);
    }

    read_status = access(filepath, R_OK);
    write_status = access(filepath, W_OK);
    // Checks for the both Read and Write Access
    if(read_status == 0 && write_status == 0){
```

```
        printf("%s File has both read and write permissions\n", filepath);
    }else if(read_status == 0 && write_status == -1){
        // If file has only read access then
        printf("%s File has only read permissions\n", filepath);
    }else if(read_status == -1 && write_status == 0){
        // If file has only write access then
        printf("%s File has only write permissions\n", filepath);
    }else{
        // If file does not have both read and write access then
    printf("%s File has no read and write permissions", filepath);
    }

    return 0;
}
```

This program tests the read and write access of a file and prints the output (i.e., read or write). You can modify the code to test execute permissions as well.

Soft and Hard Links

A link is a pointer to a file in the Unix system. In Linux, everything is considered a file, which has an inode number. A link acts as a shortcut to quickly access it. This happens because the link either points to the original file or its inode number. This helps the link provide faster access to the content. There are two types of links available in Linux: soft links and hard links.

Soft Links

A *soft link* links to a file, which contains data. There may be more than one soft link for a single file.

- It is also called a *symbolic link*.

- Different inode numbers and permissions are set for a link. A soft link offers easy access to the original file because it directly points to the original.

- Soft links can be created for files and directories in the system.

- Permissions are not updated in a soft link. Permissions are updated in the main file, but the soft link permissions are not updated. This is one of the weird behaviors of soft links.

- The changes that are made to the original file are updated. All the changes made to the soft link file are updated to the main file.

A diagram of symbolic links is shown in Figure 4-5.

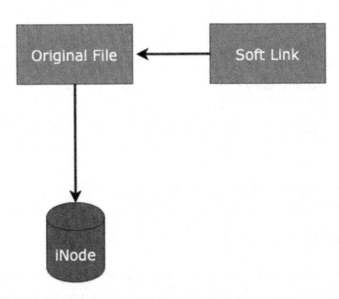

Figure 4-5. *Soft link internal connection*

Creating a Soft Link Using the Command Line

The creation of a soft link is done with the ln command and some extra flags. Let's look at creating a soft link.

```
ln -s <file_name> <softlink_name>
```

Note   The soft link name is your choice; there are no restrictions on for user's name.

Figure 4-6 shows an example.

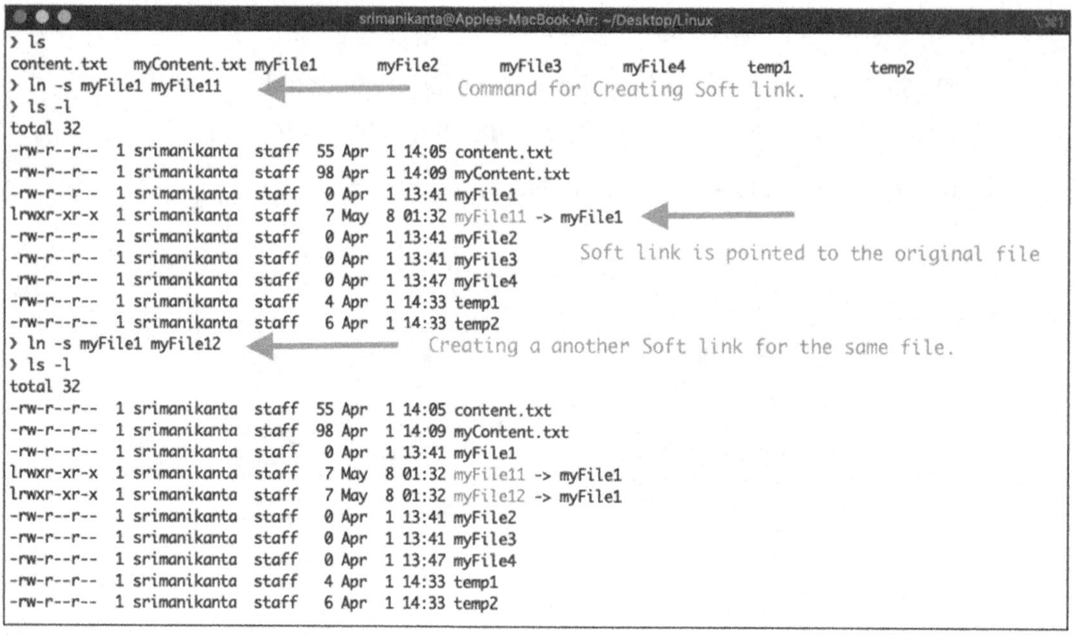

Figure 4-6. *Soft link creation using command line*

Unlinking a Soft Link

When a soft link is created, a link file is too. There are two ways to remove these links from the file.

- Delete the link file

  rm <soft_link_name>

- Unlink the file

  unlink <soft_link_name>

After the unlinking action is done, the soft link is no longer available in the system. Let's closely look at the example shown in Figure 4-7.

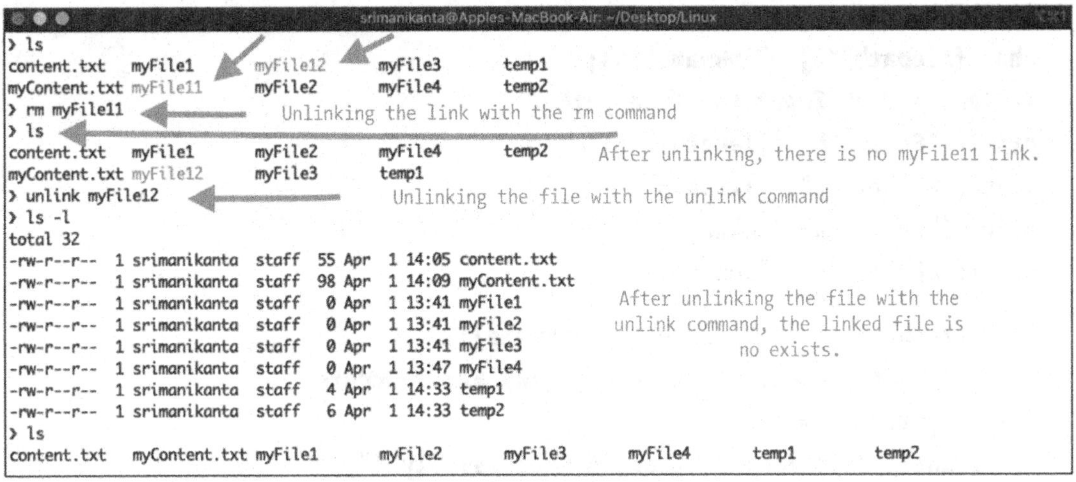

Figure 4-7. *Unlinking the soft link using a command line*

Creating a Soft Link Using System Calls

You can programmatically create symbolic or soft links. In the unistd.h library, there is a system call named symlink that creates symbolic links effectively. The symlink function returns an integer value. It returns 0 on the successful creation of a symbolic link; it returns –1 if any failure occurs.

The following shows the syntax.

```
int symlink(const char *filepath,
            const char *linkname);
```

- **filepath** takes its name as an argument where the file is located in the system.

- **linkname** takes the link name as an argument. You can also use the path where you want to store it.

Now let's programmatically create a symbolic link in a simple way.

```
#include<stdio.h>
#include<unistd.h>

int main(){
```

```
    int link_status;
    char filepath[50], linkname[50];
    // Taking User Input for file path
    printf("Enter the filepath: ");
    scanf("%[^\n]%*c", filepath);
    printf("Enter the linkname: ");
    scanf("%[^\n]%*c", linkname);

    link_status = symlink(filepath,linkname);
    // 0 ---> On Success || -1 ---> If Any Error Occurs
    if(link_status == 0){
        printf("Soft link is Created Successfully.!");
    }else{
        printf("Unable to Create the Link.");
    }

    return 0;
}
```

This program creates a soft link and returns a success statement if there is success and failure messages if any error occurs.

Unlinking Using a System Call

The unlink function unlinks a link. It is available in the unistd.h library. It returns an integer value: 0 if successful and –1 if any failure occurs.

The following shows the syntax.

```
int unlink(const char *pathname);
```

> pathname takes the link path as an argument and unlinks the pointer from the original file.

Let's look at unlinking a pointer from a file in a simple way.

```
#include<stdio.h>
#include<unistd.h>

int main(){
```

```
int unlink_status;
char linkname[100];

// Taking the Link name as Input from the user to unlink
printf("Enter the link name to unlink:");
scanf("%[^\n]%*c", linkname);

unlink_status = unlink(linkname);
// 0 --->On Success || -1 ---> Failure.
if(unlink_status == 0){
    printf("File is unlinked Successfully.!");
}else{
    printf("Unable to unlink the file.");
}

    return 0;
}
```

This program unlinks the file from the pointer. It does the same as the command rm, and unlink does. On successful unlinking of a pointer, it returns the successful message. On an unsuccessful unlink, it returns a failure message.

Hard Links

A *hard link* is a mirror copy of the original file. If you accidentally delete the original file, the data remains in the hard link file, since it is a mirror copy of the original file. The following are some of the implications.

- The data updated on the original file is reflected on the hard link.

- It works only on a single file system, which means that it can't create hard links for other operating system file systems.

- It can't link to directories.

- It has the same inode number and permissions as the original file.

Figure 4-8 is a diagram of a hard link.

Hard Link Internal Connection

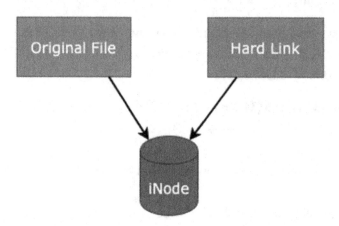

Figure 4-8. *Hard link internal connection*

Creating a Hard Link Using the Command Line

The creation of a hard link is done with the ln command. The link and the original file have the same data, permissions, and inode number.

ln <filename> <hard_link_name>

Here's an example.

```
srimanikanta@Apples-MacBook-Air: ~/Desktop/Linux
> vi LinkData          ←——    Created a file with raw content
> ln LinkData CreatedHardLink    ←——    Created the hard link with the ln command
> ls -lia
total 40
28174395 drwxr-xr-x@ 14 srimanikanta  staff   448 May  8 02:39 .
  743375 drwx------@ 231 srimanikanta  staff  7392 May  8 01:53 ..
28175157 drwxr-xr-x   2 srimanikanta  staff    64 Apr  1 13:51 .myOwnHiddenDirectory
28175165 -rw-r--r--   1 srimanikanta  staff     0 Apr  1 13:51 .myOwnHiddenFile
31227742 -rw-r--r--   2 srimanikanta  staff    25 May  8 02:39 CreatedHardLink    The hard link and
31227742 -rw-r--r--   2 srimanikanta  staff    25 May  8 02:39 LinkData            original file have
28175708 -rw-r--r--   1 srimanikanta  staff    98 Apr  1 14:09 myContent.txt       the same inode number
28174859 -rw-r--r--   1 srimanikanta  staff     0 Apr  1 13:41 myFile1             and permissions.
28174860 -rw-r--r--   1 srimanikanta  staff     0 Apr  1 13:41 myFile2
28174861 -rw-r--r--   1 srimanikanta  staff     0 Apr  1 13:41 myFile3
28175062 -rw-r--r--   1 srimanikanta  staff     0 Apr  1 13:47 myFile4
31227716 -rw-r--r--   1 srimanikanta  staff     0 May  8 02:38 s1.txt
28176465 -rw-r--r--   1 srimanikanta  staff     4 Apr  1 14:33 temp1
28176468 -rw-r--r--   1 srimanikanta  staff     6 Apr  1 14:33 temp2
> vi CreatedHardLink    ←——    Modified some content in the hard link
> cat LinkData
This is a Original File.                              Data is reflected on
Added my Own text in Hardlink                         the original file as well
```

Figure 4-9. *Hard link creation using command line*

Creating a Hard Link Using a System Call

The creation of a hard link is done with a link system call. This system call function is available in the unistd.h library. It returns an integer value: 0 for a success and –1 for a failure.

The following shows the syntax.

```
int link(const char *filepath,
         const char *linkname);
```

- **filepath** takes its name as an argument where the file is located in the system.

- **linkname** takes the link name as an argument. You can also provide the path where you want to store it.

Here's an example.

```
#include<stdio.h>
#include<unistd.h>
int main(){
   int link_status;
   char filepath[50], linkname[50];
   printf("Enter the filename: ");
   scanf("%[^\n]%*c", filepath);
   printf("Enter the linkname: ");
   scanf("%[^\n]%*c", linkname);

   link_status = link(filepath, linkname);
   // Hardlink be Created.
   // 0 ---> Successful || -1 ---> Failure.

   if(link_status == 0){
       printf("HardLink is Created Successfully.!");
   }else{
       printf("Unable to Create the Hard Link.");
   }

   return 0;
}
```

This program creates a hard link and prints the success message if appropriate. If any error occurs, it prints a failure message.

Note   The unlinking of both the hard and soft links can be done in the same command (i.e., using either the rm command or the unlink command. Programmatically, the same unlink system call which is available in the unistd.h unlink the link that is created. Once the link is unlinked, it is deleted from the system.

System Calls for Directories

So far, various file concepts and their respective system calls have been covered. Several activities were performed programmatically. Now it's time to dig deeper into the directories and various system functions that are associated with it. Directories are frequently used in daily life to organize files in a well-structured manner. This section discussed the various system calls that are available in C programming. The following are the most common operations performed in a directory.

- Creating a directory

- Removing a directory

- Getting the current working directory

- Changing a directory

- Reading a directory

- Closing a directory

Creating a Directory

The creation of a directory is done with the mkdir function, which is available in the sys/stat.h library. The return type of this function is an integer. It returns 0 on the successful creation of a directory; it returns –1 for a failure.

The following shows the syntax.

```
int mkdir(const char *path, mode_t mode);
```

- **p**ath is the first argument that describes the path and the new directory name to create in the system.

- mode represents the permissions to give to a new directory.

Let's look at a simple example of creating a directory programmatically. The following code creates a new directory in the current program location.

```
#include<stdio.h>
#include<sys/stat.h>
#include<sys/types.h>
int main(){
    int isCreated;
    char *DIR_NAME;
    printf("Enter the Directory name you want to create: ");
    scanf("%[^\n]%*c", DIR_NAME);
 // You can Set your own permissions based on your Requirements.
    isCreated = mkdir(DIR_NAME, 0777);

    if(isCreated == 0){ // The value is 0 for Successful
        printf("Directory is Created Successfully\n");
    }else{  // Value is -1 if it is unsuccessful.
        printf("Unable to Create Directory\n");
    }

    return 0;
}
```

This creates a new directory and prints a success message if the creation operation is successful; otherwise, it prints an error message.

Deleting a Directory

The deletion of a directory is done with the rmdir function, which is available in the sys/stat.h library. The return type of this function is an integer. It returns 0 on the successful deletion of a directory; it returns –1 if a failure.

The following shows the syntax.

```
int rmdir(const char *pathname);
```

> pathname determines the directory name with the absolute path to
> remove from the system.

Let's look at an example of how to delete a directory from the system.

```
#include<stdio.h>
#include<sys/stat.h>
#include<sys/types.h>

int rmdir(char *dirname);
int main(){
    int isRemoved;
    char DIR_NAME[512];
    printf("Enter the Directory name you want to create: ");
    scanf("%[^\n]%*c", DIR_NAME);
    isRemoved = rmdir(DIR_NAME);

    if(isRemoved == 0){ // The value is 0 for Successful
        printf("Directory is Deleted Successfully\n");
    }else{  // Value is -1 if it is unsuccessful.
        printf("Unable to Delete Directory\n");
    }
    return 0;
}
```

This program deletes the directory from the system and prints a success message for
a successful operation; otherwise, it returns a failure message.

Getting the Current Working Directory

The getcwd function gets the current working directory. It is available in the unistd.h
library. The return of this function is a character data type. It returns the program's
current working directory.

The following shows the syntax.

```
char getcwd(char *buffer, size_t buffersize);
```

- buffer is the first argument; it describes the char array that stores the buffer content.

- buffersize is the second argument; it is the length of the buffer.

Let's look at a program to print the current working directory using the C program.

```
#include<stdio.h>
#include<unistd.h>
int main(){
    char DIR[75];
    printf("Current Working Directory is: %s\n", getcwd(DIR, 75));
    return 0;
}
```

This program prints the current working directory when a success; otherwise, it prints NULL.

Changing Directory

There is a chdir system call that changes directory in your operating system. It is available in the unistd.h library. The return type of this function is an integer. It returns 0 on the successful change in a directory; it returns –1 for a failure.

The following shows the syntax.

```
int chdir(const char *path);
```

path describes the path to change.

Here is a C program that changes the directory in a system.

```
#include<stdio.h>
#include<unistd.h>
int main(){

char DIR[75];
```

```
// Prints the Current Working Directory Before change
printf("Working Directory Before Operation:%s\n",
getcwd(DIR, 75));

    //The below chdir("..") change to the parent directory.
    int status = chdir("..");

    //Success ---> 0 & Failure ---> -1
    if(status == 0){
        printf("Directory Changed Successfully.!\n");
    }else{
        printf("Unable to change the Directory.\n");
    }
// Prints the Current Working Directory After change
printf("Working Directory After Operation: %s\n",
getcwd(DIR, 75));
    return 0;
}
```

This program changes the working directory of the calling process.

Reading a Directory

Two types of functions read the content in directories: opendir and readdir. They are available in the dirent.h library. The return type of the opendir function is the directory stream.

A directory stream is an ordered sequence of all directory entries in a directory. A directory entry represents the files. This directory stream points to the start position.

The return type of readdir is a dirent structure, which returns NULL if the directory reaches its end. Dirent is a built-in structure that is implemented in the dirent.h library.

The following shows the syntax.

DIR *opendir(const char *path);

- The path argument indicates the value that you want to open.

    struct dirent *readdir(DIR *directorypointer);

- The **directorypointer** argument should contain the directory stream pointer, which is a return value of the opendir function.

The internal structure of dirent is as follows.

```
struct dirent{
    ino_t           d_ino;      // inode number
    off_t           d_off;      // offset to the next dirent
    unsigned short d_reclen;    // length of this record
    unsigned char  d_type;      // type of file;
    char            d_name[256]; // filename
};
```

Let's create a program in C that reads all the files in a directory and prints them to the console.

```
#include <stdio.h>
#include<stdlib.h>
#include <dirent.h>
 int main() {
   // Directory Entry
   struct dirent *DIR_ENTRY;
    // opendir() returns a pointer of DIR type.
   DIR *DIR_READER = opendir(".");
    if (DIR_READER == NULL) {
       printf("Could not open current directory" );
       exit(1);
   }
    while ((DIR_ENTRY = readdir(DIR_READER)) != NULL)
           printf("%s\n", DIR_ENTRY->d_name);

   closedir(DIR_READER);
   return 0;
}
```

This program returns all the files and folders present in the given location.

Closing a Directory

The closedir function closes the directory stream that is running in a process. The return type of this function is an integer. It returns 0 on the successful closing of a directory; it returns –1 for a failure.

The following shows the syntax.

int closedir(DIR *directorypointer);

directorypointer is an argument that contains the directory stream pointer, which is simply a return value of the opendir function.

Here's an example.

```
#include <stdio.h>
#include<stdlib.h>
#include <dirent.h>
 int main() {
   // Directory Entry
   struct dirent *DIR_ENTRY;
    // opendir() returns a pointer of DIR type.
   DIR *DIR_READER = opendir(".");
    if (DIR_READER == NULL) {
       printf("Could not open current directory" );
       exit(1);
   }

   int status = closedir(DIR_READER);
   if(status == 0){
       printf("Directory Closed Successfully.!");
   }else{
       printf("Unable to close the Directory.");
   }
   return 0;
}
```

This program prints the success statement if the directory is closed successfully; otherwise, it prints a failure message.

Summary

This chapter focused on the Unix file structure, including the following topics.

- A file's metadata and inode structure and how the Unix system identifies a file in the system.

- The system calls that are available for file operations in the Unix system and various file I/O operations.

- How chmod() changes file permissions programmatically. The access function checks file permissions with attributes like R_OK, W_OK, F_OK, and X_OK.

- The various Linux commands to create soft and hard links, including the programmatic ways to create them. This included a discussion on unlinking a link in both command-based and programmatic ways.

- The various directory system calls that manipulate directory operations.

CHAPTER 5

Process and Signals

Processes play a major role on an operating system. When you execute a computer program in your system, it is done with a process. Without processes, you aren't able to do any activity on an OS. In this chapter, you look at processes and how to perform various tasks. You also see various types of processes that can occur during the execution of a program.

Signals are interrupts or traps (a trap is a fault) that raise an event when an exception occurs. It is very handy to be able to detect exceptions and interrupts caused by the system or a program. Signals are more helpful when working with core system-level applications. This chapter discusses the following topics.

- Introduction to process environments

- Linux subsystems

- Process creation

- A zombie process

- An orphan process

- System calls for process management

- Signals and their types

- System calls for signal management

© Sri Manikanta Palakollu 2021
S. M. Palakollu, *Practical System Programming with C*, https://doi.org/10.1007/978-1-4842-6321-1_5

Introduction to the Process Environment

An executing program is considered a process. To get a deeper understanding of a process, you need to be familiar with the process environment. Let's consider the internal working mechanisms of a normal C program that is subjected to the kernel for execution. You are already know that every C program execution starts with the main() function; but behind the scenes, a special start-up routine is called by the kernel before calling the main() function.

When you compile C code, an executable is generated by the compiler. This executable program contains the starting address of the start-up routine set up by the linker when the program is executed. But when ASLR (address space layout randomization) is enabled, the startup routine address is unpredictable. ASLR is a memory protection mechanism that resolves buffer overflow issues by randomizing the location. This startup routine usually takes a kernel. That type of argument is called a *command-line argument*.

Let's start with some basics and work toward a deeper understanding. A typical C program main function look likes the following.

int main(int argc, char *argv[]);

It contains two parameters that take command-line arguments.

- **argc** takes an integer type as an argument that contains the number of command-line arguments passed by the programmer. The parameters that are passing to the command line should be space separated. This means if you pass *hello world*, it is considered two different arguments, but hello_world is a single argument. If you want to pass a spaced single argument, it is advisable to pass it inside double quotes (i.e., "hello world"), which is also considered a single argument.

- **argv** takes a character array type as an argument. It deals with the array of pointers that point to the argument values.

Let's look at a simple C program that prints all the command-line values that are passed by the programmer explicitly.

#include<stdio.h>
int main(int argc, char * argv[]){

```
printf("Number of Arguments Passed: %d\n", argc);
// This loop prints the all the command line values
// that are passed through the program.
for(int i=0;i<argc;i++){
    printf("%s\n", argv[i]);
}

return 0;
}
```

The output of the program look like Figure 5-1.

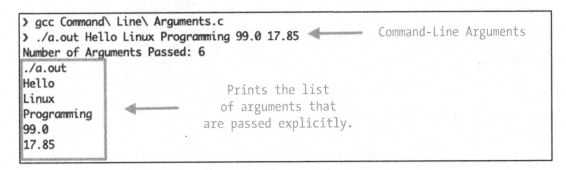

Figure 5-1. *Output of C program for command-line arguments*

The program is named "Command\ Line\ Arguments.c". The gcc compiler compiles this program. After the compilation is done, the programmer run the program. This program was run with five types of command-line values. A loop to print all the command-line values was written. This program prints all the passed arguments and the number of arguments. There is an odd behavior that you can observe in the output: there were six arguments passed because it counted the executable file value as well.

Environment List

Your operating system has an environment list of items stored in an array of character pointers. A process environment has an environment list. An *environ* is a character pointer variable that points to an environment list. You can access this variable data with the extern keyword. The syntax is as follows; also see Figure 5-2.

extern char **environ;

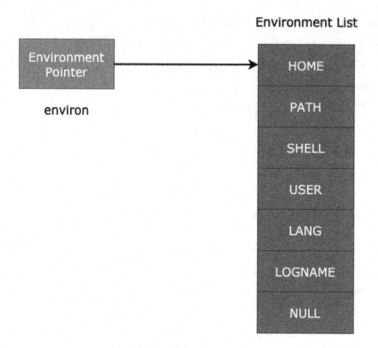

Figure 5-2. *Environment variables list*

- Environ is an environment pointer that points to the environment list, which consists of string data.

- The environment list consists of predefined variables and custom process variables. All the predefined values are in uppercase format.

- The format of an environment list is name=value.

- The executing program is also present under this environment list variable.

Here's an example.

```
#include<stdio.h>

int main(){

    extern char **environ;
    char **environment_list = environ;

    /* This code Helps us to prints the all the
       Environments available in the operating system.
    */
```

```
    while(*environment_list != NULL){
        printf("%s\n", *environment_list);
        environment_list++;
    }

    return 0;
}
```

This program prints all the environment variables in your operating system and the variables defined in your current session/program. The list of values that are printed by the program contain your program execution file as well.

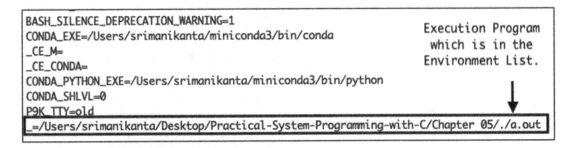

Figure 5-3. *Output of the environment variable list using C program*

This program shows the predefined and working process items listed in the environment list. Finally, you can see the program execution path, which is assigned to the _ variable. The running program's instance is available in a running processes list. This proves every program under execution is considered a process.

Memory Layout of a C Program

The memory layout of a C program typically consists of various block items. Each block has a specific task to do within the running program. To get a clear view of the memory layout in a C program, let's look at memory layout in the pictorial representation shown in Figure 5-4.

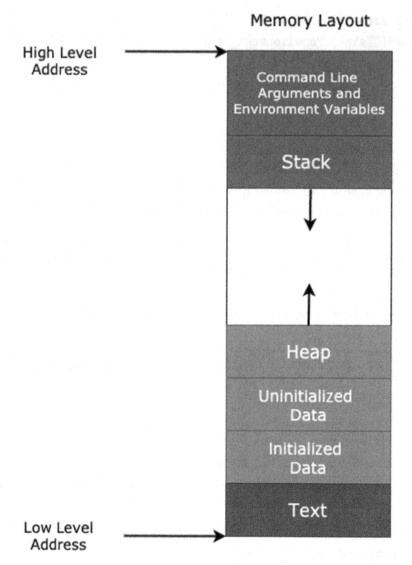

Figure 5-4. *Memory layout*

The entire memory layout is divided into several blocks. Each block has a separate functionality associated with it.

Command-Line Arguments

The command-line argument block accepts all the values explicitly passed by the programmer. This block also contains environment variables.

Stack

A *stack* is used for static allocation in a program. It stores all the automatic variables. The function call's results are stored in the stack area, but you can't estimate or predict exactly where a function call's results will store. It depends on the hardware architecture. Function call results are ABI (application binary interface) dependent. The values stored in the stack are directly stored in RAM (random-access memory). Access time for items in the stack space is very fast.

Heap

A *heap* is used for dynamic memory allocation. Allocation of memory is done at runtime and accessing the items present in a heap space is slower than in a stack space. The size of the heap is limited to the size of your virtual memory.

Uninitialized Data

The kernel assigns the data present in this segmented block to an arithmetic zero or the NULL pointer before the program starts executing. This block is also called a *BSS block*, which is a *block started by symbol*. Global and static variables that don't have any explicit initialization in the program are stored in this data block. This block contains only uninitialized data.

Initialized Data

Global and static variables initialized by the programmer with predefined values in the program are stored in the initialized data block.

Text

The text block contains the machine code/instructions the CPU needs to execute.

Process Termination Methodologies

A process is terminated normally or abnormally based on the program flow or unexpected interrupts. The termination of a process is done in the following ways.

- When a main() function returns the value, the process is terminated.

- When you call an exit() function, which is available in the stdlib.h library, to terminate a process.

- When you call the _Exit() or _exit() functions available in stdlib.h and unistd.h, respectively, to terminate a process.

- When you call pthread_exit to terminate the process.

- When you call an abort() function to abnormally terminate the process.

- When the programmer raises a signal, the process is terminated abnormally if the custom handler or built-in signal handler is not available. But you can handle the signals with a custom/built-in signal handler.

- Thread cancellation requests are also responsible for process termination. A thread cancellation request is the termination of a thread before its job is done in the process.

- Any I/O failure/interrupt leads to process termination. For example, if the process is waiting for input from a scanner but the scanner is not working, this leads to process termination. If there is any custom exception handler code available, this situation is handled easily without the process being terminated.

- In some situations, a child process is terminated because of a parent process request.

- A process is terminated when it is trying to access unallocated or unauthorized resources. For example, when a process tries to execute a program that doesn't have execution permissions, it leads to process termination. When a program tries to access memory that it does not own, it leads to process termination.

The process environment consists of the environment List, memory layout, and process termination. Memory layout deals with how program data is organized in the system memory for better access. In contrast, an environment list deals with storing all the processes that are running on an operating system. Finally, process termination methodologies terminate a process normally or abnormally, based on the programmer's requirements. Abnormally terminating a process is done when something unexpectedly happens to a program, so the programmer kills the process abnormally.

Environment Variables

Every process has an environment block that contains environment variables. An environment variable is a dynamic variable that deals with the processes and programs in an operating system.

Every operating system has an environment list and variables. These variables store the system process data/system-related path data. The operations that perform in environment variables are create, modify, delete, and save. There are two types of environment variables.

- User-level environment variables

- System-level environment variables

User-Level Environment Variables

User-level environment variables belong to a specific user in an operating system.

System-Level Environment Variable

The variables in a system-level environment can be accessed by every user in the system.

Environment Variable Examples

Table 5-1 shows some of the predefined system-level variables available in every Linux/Unix-based operating system.

Table 5-1. *List of Environment Variables*

Variable	Description
PWD	It prints the present working directory.
HOME	It prints the default path to the user's home directory.
SHELL	It prints the location of the shell used by the user.
UID	It prints the user's unique ID.
HOSTNAME	It displays the computer's hostname.

Accessing an Environment Variable

To read a value variable, you need to pass the command to the terminal as follows.

Syntax → echo $VARIABLE_NAME

Example → echo $HOME

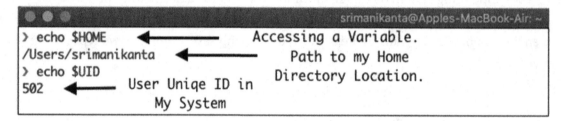

Figure 5-5. *Accessing environment variables using CLI (command-line interface)*

Note   Variable names are case sensitive. You need to be very careful when accessing data from a variable. The name needs to match exactly to get data from the system.

Setting a New Environment Variable

You can create your own environment variables with the following syntax.

Syntax → VAR_NAME=VALUE

Example → MY_VARIABLE=/Users/Home

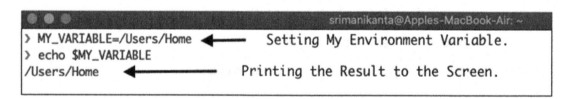

Figure 5-6. *Creating environment variable using CLI*

Note   The key point to remember in declaring a variable is that there is no space between the variable name and the value, as shown in the syntax. If there is a space between the name and the value, an error is thrown.

In bash, there is a built-in command named *export.* If you want to set the environment variable permanently, the export command is useful. This method sets the environment variable for temporary purposes only. It is not available once the terminal session is closed. The export command exports the variable to the permanent system environment variables list, which is not deleted until you delete it explicitly.

Deleting Environment Variables

Deleting an environment variable is done with the unset command.

    Syntax → unset VARIABLE_NAME
    Example → unset MY_VARIABLE

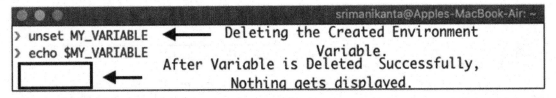

Figure 5-7. *Deleting environment variable using CLI*

Note   If you try to access an environment variable that was deleted, you get NULL as a result.

Accessing Environment Variables in C

C provides a built-in getenv() function that retrieves system variable information in a C program. The return type of this function is a pointer to the value in the environment. It takes the character value as an argument and returns the results if there is a variable in the environment list; otherwise, it prints the NULL value. This function is available in the stdlib.h library.

```
char *getenv(const char *name);
```

Here's an example.

```c
#include<stdio.h>
#include<stdlib.h>

int main(){

    char environment_name[50];
    printf("Enter the Environment name: ");
    scanf("%s", environment_name);

    printf("Environment Value: %s\n", getenv(environment_name));


    return 0;

}
```

Figure 5-8 shows the output.

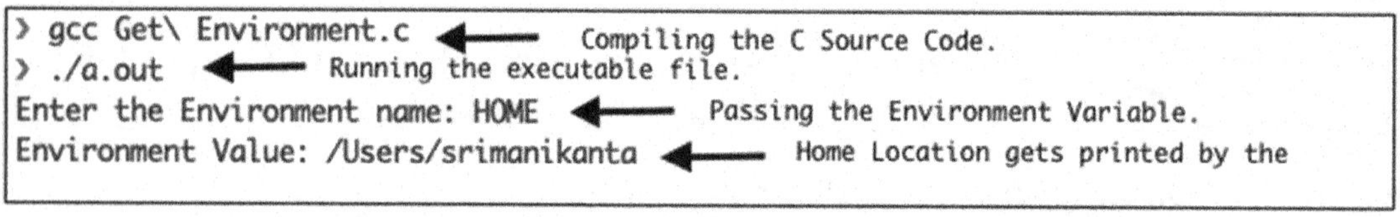

```
> gcc Get\ Environment.c  ◀——  Compiling the C Source Code.
> ./a.out  ◀——  Running the executable file.
Enter the Environment name: HOME  ◀——  Passing the Environment Variable.
Environment Value: /Users/srimanikanta  ◀——  Home Location gets printed by the
```

Figure 5-8. *Printing the environment variable using C*

Setting a New Environment Variable Using C

C provides a built-in function named setenv() that creates a new environment variable. It is available in the stdlib.h library. The return type of this function is an integer. It returns 0 for the successful creation of an environment variable; it returns –1 for any errors.

```c
int setenv(const char *envname,
           const char *envval,
           int overwrite);
```

- envname takes the name of the variable that you want to create as an environment variable.

- **envval** takes the environment variable value that you want to assign to the created value.

- **overwrite** takes the integer value as argument (i.e., either 0 or 1). A 0 doesn't overwrite an existing variable value; 1 overwrites the value. If the variable already exists in the environment, a non-zero value overwrites it.

Here's an example.

```c
#include<stdio.h>
#include<stdlib.h>

int main(){

    char variable_name[15];
    char variable_value[255];
    int overwrittenValue;
    printf("Enter your Variable name:");
    scanf("%s", variable_name);
    printf("Enter the Variable Value: ");
    scanf("%s", variable_value);

    // 1 ---> Represents the Overridden of Value.
    // 0 ---> Doesn't override the value
    printf("Enter the Overridden Value: ");
    scanf("%d", &overwrittenValue);

    // Returns 0 --> On Success || -1 on failure
    int status = setenv(variable_name, variable_value, overwrittenValue);

    if(status == 0){
        printf("Environment variable Created Successfully.!\n");
    }else if(status == -1){
        printf("Environment variable Created Successfully.!\n");
    }

    return 0;
}
```

Figure 5-9 shows the output.

```
> gcc Environment\ Variable\ Creation.c
> ./a.out
Enter your Variable name:TEST_VAR  ←——————————  Environment Variable Name.
Enter the Variable Value: /Users/Srimanikanta/Algorithms  ←————  Environment Variable Value.
Enter the Overridden Value: 1  ←————————  Overriden Value 1 for true and 0 for false.
Environment variable Created Succesfully.!  ←————  Environment Variable Created Successfully.
```

Figure 5-9. *Output of environment variable creation in C*

The successful creation of a variable prints a successful message; otherwise, an error message prints.

Deleting an Environment Variable

C provides a built-in function named unsetenv() to clear the environment variable. It is available in the stdlib.h library. The return type of this function is an integer. It returns 0 on the successful deletion of the variable; otherwise, it returns –1.

int unsetenv(const char *name);

The **name** variable takes the environment variable name, which you want to delete. Here's an example.

```
#include<stdio.h>
#include<stdlib.h>

int main(){

    char variable_name[50];
    printf("Enter the variable to Delete:");
    scanf("%s",variable_name);
    // Returns 0 --> On Success || -1 on failure
    int status = unsetenv(variable_name);

    if(status == 0){
        printf("Environment Variable is Deleted Successfully.!\n");
    }else{
        printf("Unable to Delete the Environment variable.\n");
    }

    return 0;
}
```

Figure 5-10 shows the output.

```
> gcc Environment\ Variable\ Deletion.c
> ./a.out
Enter the variable to Delete:TEST_VAR ◄──────  Deleting the previously created
Environment Variable is Deleted Successfully.!  Environment variable using setenv().
```

Figure 5-10. *Output of environment variable deletion using C*

Kernel Support for Processes

The kernel is the most important component. It manages all the operations in an operating system. The kernel handles process management and file management as well. In modern computers, multiple processes run simultaneously to execute user tasks and system tasks. These processes require several resources, which include memory, processor time, and hardware resources. The tasks and activities that are done through a kernel are depicted in Figure 5-11.

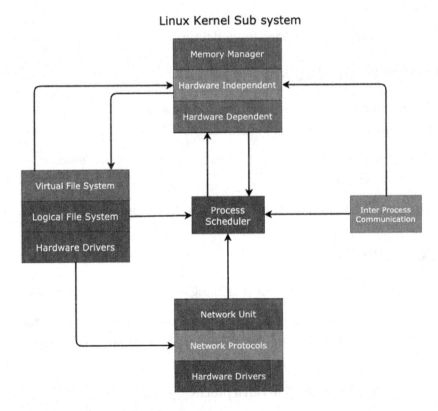

Figure 5-11. *Linux kernel-level subsystem*

Process Scheduler

The process scheduler schedules programs that are constantly running in the OS and delivers resources within a minimum response time to all programs. This is done with scheduling algorithms. The process scheduler uses two types of algorithms.

- Preemptive scheduling algorithm
- Non-preemptive scheduling algorithm

Preemptive Scheduling Algorithm

- In a preemptive scheduling algorithm, the process is interrupted before the completion of the process task.
- Starvation occurs after adding a high-priority process to the queue.
- CPU utilization is high in preemptive scheduling. In preemptive scheduling, you can keep the CPU as busy as possible with multiple processes.
- Resources are allocated for a limited time.

Non-Preemptive Scheduling Algorithm

- In a non-preemptive scheduling algorithm, a process is not interrupted until its task are finished.
- CPU utilization is low. The CPU does not allow other processes to utilize resources.
- The process utilizes resources until the task is done.

Memory Manager

The *memory manager* is responsible for managing memory in the operating system.

- It deals with the implementation of virtual memory, demand paging, and memory allocation for kernel-level space and user-level space programs.
- It maps the files required to run a process.
- It effectively manages interprocess communication tasks.

Virtual File System

A *virtual file system* is an abstract layer of a concrete file system.

- It acts as a bridge between various file systems, like Windows and macOS. This file system easily communicates with other OS file systems.

- It accesses different types of files from various file systems in a uniform way.

- It transparently handles data from network storage devices.

Network Unit

A *network unit* handles all network activities in the system.

- It manages certain types of protocols used by network hardware to transfer data between systems.

- It manages all the network hardware drivers in a system to establish effective communication.

Process Creation

Creating your own process within a program is done with a fork() system call. A newly created process is called a child process, and the process that is initiated to create the new process is considered a parent process. When a fork() system call creates a process, it creates two processes (i.e., parent and child). The diagram shown in Figure 5-12 indicates that the parent process/main process calls the fork() system call to create a process. By default, two subprocesses are created (i.e., parent and child process). A process may create another process for specific work. The creation process is called a *parent process*, and the created processes are called *child processes*. A parent process can have many child processes, but a child process has only one parent process.

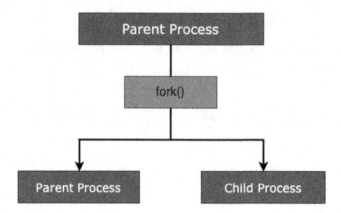

Figure 5-12. *Mechanism of process creation*

The process created to perform particular operations does a specific job in its life cycle. Before the creation of the process done, it undergoes four steps.

1. Programmer requests the process be created by the program

2. System initialization

3. Batch job initialization

4. Execution of the fork() system call by the running process

The built-in fork() system call creates its own process. The return type of this system call is an integer. It returns the three types of values. If the child process is created successfully, it returns 0. The fork() system call internally creates a copy of the process that calls it. If the parent process is successfully created, it returns a positive value. If the process is unable to create it, a negative value is returned. The syntax of the fork() system call is

int fork(void)

The internal workings of the fork() system call is demonstrated in the diagram shown in Figure 5-13. The fork() system call returns one of three values: a negative value for an error, a zero for creating a child process, and a positive value for creating a parent process. When the process ID is zero, the child process is executed, and the parent process is in a waiting state. After the child process execution is completed, the parent resumes the execution. This doesn't mean that the parent process always waits for the child process to complete its execution. You can make the parent process wait for the child process execution. The parent process terminates once its assigned work is completed. The hierarchy may vary from program to program. All the created processes share the same memory allocated to the program but have a different address space. Figure 5-13 is a simple example of creating a process using the fork() system call.

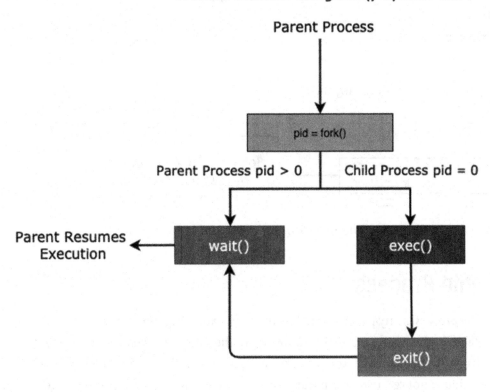

Figure 5-13. *Internal mechanism of fork() system call*

When a process is created with a fork() system call, two processes (i.e., child and copy of the parent processes) are created. When the main program creates parent and child processes, they try to execute simultaneously. This achieves concurrency in the program.

Here's an example.

```
#include <stdio.h>
#include <unistd.h>

int main() {
```

```
int pid = fork();

if(pid > 0){
    printf("Parent Process is created\n");
}else if(pid == 0){
    printf("Child Process is created\n");
 }
 return 0;
}
```

Figure 5-14 shows the output.

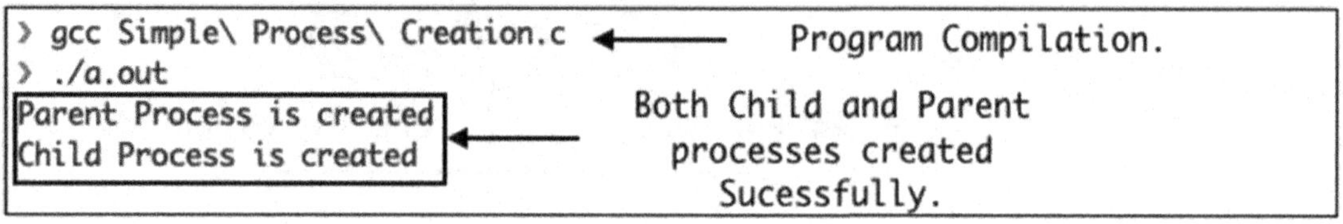

```
> gcc Simple\ Process\ Creation.c  ◄────      Program Compilation.
> ./a.out
Parent Process is created          Both Child and Parent
Child Process is created  ◄────     processes created
                                      Sucessfully.
```

Figure 5-14. *Output of the program on process creation using C*

Zombie Process

A *zombie process* is any process that has finished executing, but entry to the process is available in the process table for reporting to the parent process. A *process table* is a data structure that stores all the process-related information in an operating system. A process that is not removed from the process table is considered a zombie. The parent process removes the process entry with the exit status of the child process.

Here's an example.

```
#include<stdio.h>
#include <unistd.h>
#include <stdlib.h>
#include <sys/types.h>

int main() {

  pid_t child_pid = fork();
```

```c
// Parent process
if (child_pid > 0){
    printf("In Parent Process.!\n");
    // Making the Parent Process to Sleep for some time.
    sleep(10);
}else{
    printf("In Child process.!\n");
    exit(0);
}
  return 0;
}
```

In this program, the fork() function creates a new child process. If the child_process value is greater than zero, it is a parent process. If the child process ID is equal to zero, it is a child process. If it is a child process, the program is terminated; otherwise, the parent process is under execution in a sleep state. Meanwhile, the child process is terminated, but the process ID is in the process table, making the child process a zombie.

Orphan Process

A process that does not have a parent process is an *orphan process*. A child process becomes an orphan when either of the following occurs.

- When the task of the parent process finishes and terminates without terminating the child process.

- When an abnormal termination occurs in the parent process.

Here's an example.

```c
#include<stdio.h>
#include <unistd.h>
#include <stdlib.h>
#include <sys/types.h>

int main() {

    pid_t child_pid = fork();
```

```
// Parent process
if (child_pid > 0){
    printf("In Parent Process.!\n");

}else{
    printf("In Child process.!\n");
    // Making the Child Process to Sleep for some time.
    sleep(10);
    printf("After Sleep Time");
}
  return 0;
}
```

In this program, the parent process completes its execution and exits while the child process is in execution, so it is considered an orphan process. If there is no parent for a process, then that process is adopted by the init process.

System Calls for Process Management

When you are working with a process for a task, it is good to know how to manage the processes effectively. Until now, you have seen fork() system calls create a process. This section looks at various types of system calls that manage process activities effectively. The following system calls manage processes.

- vfork

- exec

- wait

- waitpid

- kill

- exit

- _Exit

vfork System Call

A vfork system call creates a new process, but the behavior is undefined in certain circumstances. If the process is created using a vfork system call, the parent process is blocked until the child block is executed. In the vfork system call, the child process shares a common address space as the current calling process. Since they share the common address space, changes in the code are visible to other processes. The return type of this system call is an integer. When a child is successfully created, it returns 0 and the child process ID to the parent process. If any error occurs, it returns –1.

The following shows the syntax.

pid_t vfork(void)

It takes zero arguments but creates the child process and blocks the parent process. Here's an example.

```
#include<stdio.h>
#include<unistd.h>
#include<stdlib.h>

int main(){

    pid_t status;
    status = vfork();
    printf("Process is Executing: %d\n", getpid());
    if(status == 0){
        printf("Process is executing: %d\n", getpid());
        exit(0);
    }

    return 0;
}
```

This code explains the working mechanisms of the vfork system call. Initially, the child process is created and executes its task after the parent process is executed.

```
❯ gcc vfork.c                                          5936 - Child PID
❯ ./a.out                                              5935 - Parent PID
Process is Executing: 5936 ◄──────── Child process is Executing the Statements.
Process is executing: 5936
Process is Executing: 5935 ◄─────  Parent process is Executing
```

Figure 5-15. Output of process creation using vfork() system call

---

Note   The vfork() system call is removed from POSIX standards due to its undefined behavior in certain circumstances.

---

exec System Call Family

The exec system call family replaces the currently running process with a new process. But the original process identifier remains the same, and all the internal details, such as stack, data, and instructions. The new process replaces the executables. This function call family runs binary executables and shell scripts. Figure 5-16 shows the workings of the exec system call.

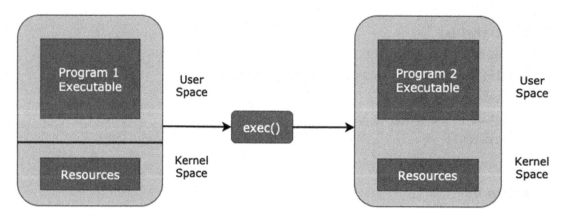

Figure 5-16. Working mechanism of exec system call

There are several system calls of the same family type available in the unistd.h library. They create a new process or execute another binary executable. The family of the exec system call functions include the following.

- execl

- execlp

- execle

- execv

- execvp

- execve

execl( )

This system call takes the first and second parameter as a path of the binary executable. and the remaining parameters are the ones that you need to pass as based on your interest; that is, optional parameters or flags that are required for the executable program and purpose followed by a NULL value. This system call is available in the unistd.h library. The return type of this function is an integer. If the execution is unsuccessful, it returns –1; otherwise, it returns nothing.

The following shows the syntax.

int execl(const char *path, const char *arg, ..., NULL)

- path takes the binary executable with the complete path.

- arg also takes the binary executable path as an argument.

- [...] considers the variable number of arguments, which means you can pass any number of arguments.

- NULL is the default parameter, which the execl function's last parameter should be.

Here's an example.

```
#include <unistd.h>
int main() {

  char *binary_path = "/bin/ls";
  char *arg1 = "-l";
  char *arg2 = "-a";
  char *arg3 = ".";
```

```
// System call to perform the ls -la operation in the
// CWD (Current Working Directory)
execl(binary_path, binaryPath, arg1, arg2, arg3, NULL);
return 0;
}
```

This program shows a long list of all the files and directories, including the hidden ones and the execl system call (see Figure 5-17). The advantage of this program is that with one process identifier, another process is also executed.

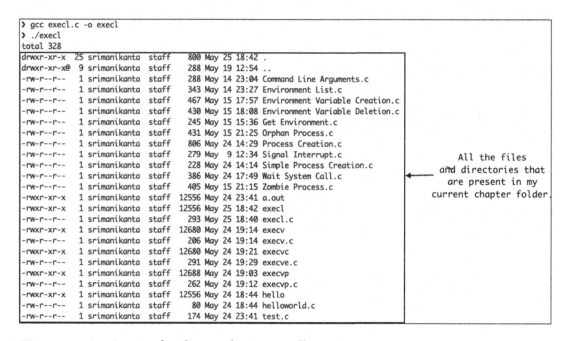

Figure 5-17. *Output for the execl system call*

execlp( )

This system call is a bit more advanced than the execl() system call. It does not require the path for the binary built-in executable, but for custom executables, it does require the path to execute. The return type of this system call is an integer. It returns –1 if any error occurs and returns anything for successful execution.

The following shows the syntax.

int execlp(const char *path, const char *arg, ..., NULL)

- **path** takes the binary executable with the complete path.

- arg also takes the binary executable path as an argument.

- [...] considers the variable number of arguments, which means you can pass any number of arguments.

- NULL is the default parameter, which the execl function's last parameter should be.

Here's an example.

```
#include <unistd.h>
int main() {

 char *binary_executable = "ls";
 char *arg1 = "-la";
 char *arg2 = ".";
  // System call to perform the ls -la operation in the
  // CWD (Current Working Directory)
 execlp(binary_executable, binary_executable, arg1, arg2, NULL);
 return 0;
}
```

The output of this program is the same as the execl() system call program that prints the long listing of the current working directory (see Figure 5-18).

```
> gcc execlp.c -o execlp
> ./execlp
total 368
drwxr-xr-x  27 srimanikanta  staff    864 May 25 18:56 .
drwxr-xr-x@  9 srimanikanta  staff    288 May 25 18:50 ..
-rw-r--r--   1 srimanikanta  staff    288 May 14 23:04 Command Line Arguments.c
-rw-r--r--   1 srimanikanta  staff    343 May 14 23:27 Environment List.c
-rw-r--r--   1 srimanikanta  staff    467 May 15 17:57 Environment Variable Creation.c
-rw-r--r--   1 srimanikanta  staff    430 May 15 18:08 Environment Variable Deletion.c
-rw-r--r--   1 srimanikanta  staff    245 May 15 15:36 Get Environment.c
-rw-r--r--   1 srimanikanta  staff    431 May 15 21:25 Orphan Process.c
-rw-r--r--   1 srimanikanta  staff    806 May 24 14:29 Process Creation.c
-rw-r--r--   1 srimanikanta  staff    279 May  9 12:34 Signal Interrupt.c
-rw-r--r--   1 srimanikanta  staff    228 May 24 14:14 Simple Process Creation.c
-rw-r--r--   1 srimanikanta  staff    386 May 24 17:49 Wait System Call.c
-rw-r--r--   1 srimanikanta  staff    405 May 15 21:15 Zombie Process.c
-rwxr-xr-x   1 srimanikanta  staff  12556 May 24 23:41 a.out
-rwxr-xr-x   1 srimanikanta  staff  12556 May 25 18:42 execl
-rw-r--r--   1 srimanikanta  staff    295 May 25 18:49 execl.c
-rwxr-xr-x   1 srimanikanta  staff  12556 May 25 18:56 execlp
-rw-r--r--   1 srimanikanta  staff    315 May 25 18:56 execlp.c
-rwxr-xr-x   1 srimanikanta  staff  12680 May 24 19:14 execv
-rw-r--r--   1 srimanikanta  staff    206 May 24 19:14 execv.c
-rwxr-xr-x   1 srimanikanta  staff  12680 May 24 19:21 execvc
-rw-r--r--   1 srimanikanta  staff    291 May 24 19:29 execve.c
-rwxr-xr-x   1 srimanikanta  staff  12688 May 24 19:03 execvp
-rw-r--r--   1 srimanikanta  staff    262 May 24 19:12 execvp.c
-rwxr-xr-x   1 srimanikanta  staff  12556 May 25 18:50 hello
-rw-r--r--   1 srimanikanta  staff     80 May 24 18:44 helloworld.c
-rw-r--r--   1 srimanikanta  staff    174 May 24 23:41 test.c
```

Long listing of the files and the directories in the chapter working directory.

Figure 5-18. *Output for execlp() system call*

execle( )

This system call works similarly to the execl() system call. The major difference is that you can pass your own environment variables as an array. You can access the environment variables from the envp constant array pointer. The return type of this system call is an integer. It returns –1 on an error and returns anything for the successful execution of the executable.

The following shows the syntax.

```
int execle(const char *path,
           const char *arg,
           ..., NULL,
           char * const envp[])
```

- **path** takes the binary executable with the complete path.

- **arg** also takes the binary executable path as an argument.

- [...] considers the variable number of arguments, which means you can pass any number of arguments.

- **NULL** is the default parameter, which the execl function's last parameter should be.

- **envp** is an environment pointer variable that lets you access the environment variables from the array. The last element of the array is a NULL value.

Here's an example.

```
#include <unistd.h>

int main() {

 char *binary_path = "/bin/zsh";
 char *arg1 = "-c";
 char *arg2 = "echo \"Visit $HOSTNAME:$PORT from your browser.\"";
 char *const envp[] = {"HOSTNAME=www.netflix.com", "PORT=80", NULL};
    // execle() System call can able to access
    // the envp environment variables.

 execle(binary_path, binary_path, arg1, arg2, NULL, envp);
 return 0;
}
```

The output for this code is a statement to visit the URL in the browser. This is done by accessing the environment variables with the echo statement within a C program.

```
> gcc execle.c -o execle                    Printing the Statement
> ./execle                           to the Console by Accessing the
Visit www.netflix.com:80 from your browser. ←    Environment Variables.
```

Figure 5-19. *Output for execle() system call*

execv()

This execv() system call is slightly different from this all three system calls. In this system call you can pass your parameters as an argv array that you want to execute. The last element of this array is a NULL value. The return type of this system call is an integer value. It returns –1 on an error and returns nothing on success.

The following shows the syntax.

int execv(const char *path, char *const argv[])

- The path argument points to the path of the executable that is being executed.

- argv is the second argument. It is a NULL-terminated array of character pointers.

Here's an example.

```
#include<stdio.h>
#include<unistd.h>

int main() {

    //A null terminated array of character pointers
    char *args[]={"./hello",NULL};
    execv(args[0],args);

    return 0;
}
```

In this code, when execv() system call is executed, it calls the ./hello binary executable, which contains the simple hello world program, and is executed.

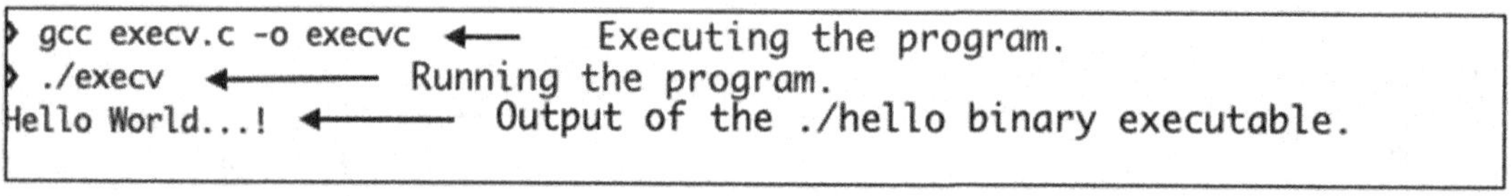

```
> gcc execv.c -o execvc ←——      Executing the program.
> ./execv ←———————— Running the program.
Hello World...! ←———————— Output of the ./hello binary executable.
```

Figure 5-20. *Output for execv() system call*

execvp()

This system call works the as same as the execv() system call. The major difference is that you don't need to pass the path for system executables like an execlp() system call. The execvp() system call tries to find the path of the file in an operating system.

In the following example, the ls command is a program name. The execvp() system call automatically finds its path in the system and performs the action.

The following shows the syntax.

int execvp (const char *file, char *const argv[])

- **file** points to the executable file name associated with the file being executed.

- argv is a NULL-terminated array of character pointers that contain the executables information.

Here's an example.

```
#include<stdio.h>
#include<unistd.h>

int main() {

    char *program_name = "ls";
    //A null terminated array of character pointers
    char *args[]={program_name,"-la", ".", NULL};
    execvp(program_name,args);

    return 0;
}
```

In this code, the execvp() system call calls the built-in ls command, displaying all the contents in a directory. External parameters like -la with . means that it performs a long-list operation by displaying the hidden details of the current directory. This operation simply refers to the ls -la, where . is an external parameter that considers the current working directory of the program.

```
> gcc execvp.c -o execvp
> ./execvp
total 208
drwxr-xr-x  19 srimanikanta  staff     608 May 24 19:03 .
drwxr-xr-x@  9 srimanikanta  staff     288 May 19 12:54 ..
-rw-r--r--   1 srimanikanta  staff     288 May 14 23:04 Command Line Arguments.c
-rw-r--r--   1 srimanikanta  staff     343 May 14 23:27 Environment List.c
-rw-r--r--   1 srimanikanta  staff     467 May 15 17:57 Environment Variable Creation.c
-rw-r--r--   1 srimanikanta  staff     430 May 15 18:08 Environment Variable Deletion.c
-rw-r--r--   1 srimanikanta  staff     245 May 15 15:36 Get Environment.c
-rw-r--r--   1 srimanikanta  staff     431 May 15 21:25 Orphan Process.c
-rw-r--r--   1 srimanikanta  staff     806 May 24 14:29 Process Creation.c
-rw-r--r--   1 srimanikanta  staff     279 May  9 12:34 Signal Interrupt.c
-rw-r--r--   1 srimanikanta  staff     228 May 24 14:14 Simple Process Creation.c
-rw-r--r--   1 srimanikanta  staff     386 May 24 17:49 Wait System Call.c
-rw-r--r--   1 srimanikanta  staff     405 May 15 21:15 Zombie Process.c
-rwxr-xr-x   1 srimanikanta  staff   12736 May 24 18:42 a.out
-rw-r--r--   1 srimanikanta  staff     228 May 24 18:39 execl.c
-rwxr-xr-x   1 srimanikanta  staff   12688 May 24 19:03 execvp
-rw-r--r--   1 srimanikanta  staff     262 May 24 19:00 execvp.c
-rwxr-xr-x   1 srimanikanta  staff   12556 May 24 18:44 hello
-rw-r--r--   1 srimanikanta  staff      80 May 24 18:44 helloworld.c
```

Long Listing the details of the directory ◄— with the hidden files and directories as well.

Figure 5-21. *Output for execvp() system call*

execve( )

This system call works the same as the execle() system call. You can pass the environment variables, and those variables can access it from your program.

```
int execve(
          const char *file,
          char *const argv[],
          char *const envp[]
       )
```

Here's an example.

```
#include <unistd.h>
int main() {

 char *binary_path = "/bin/bash";
 // Argument Array
 char *const args[] = {binary_path, "-c", "echo \"Visit $HOSTNAME:$PORT
from your browser.\"", NULL};
 // Environment Variable Array
 char *const env[] = {"HOSTNAME=www.netflix.com", "PORT=80", NULL};
 execve(binary_path, args, env);
 return 0;
}
```

This code is the same as the execle() system call output, as shown in Figure 5-22.

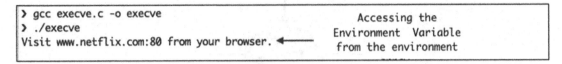

```
> gcc execve.c -o execve                          Accessing the
> ./execve                                   Environment  Variable
Visit www.netflix.com:80 from your browser. ◄─── from the environment
```

Figure 5-22. *Output for execve() system call*

wait System Call

In some situations, a process needs to wait for resources or for other processes to complete execution. A common situation that occurs during the creation of a child process is that the parent process needs to wait or suspend until the child process execution is completed. After the child process execution completes, the parent process resumes execution. The work of the wait system call is to suspend the parent system call until its child process terminates. This wait system call is available in the sys/wait.h header file. The process ID is the return type of the wait system call. On successful termination of the child process, it returns the child process ID to the parent process. If the process doesn't have any child processes, the initiated wait call does not affect the parent activity. It returns –1 if there are no child processes. If the parent process has multiple child processes, the wait() call returns the appropriate result to the parent when the child processes have terminated.

The following shows the syntax.

pid_t wait(int *status)

This system call takes the child status as an argument and returns the terminated child process ID. If you don't want to give the child status, you can use the NULL value. The workings of the wait function are shown in the Figure 5-23 diagram.

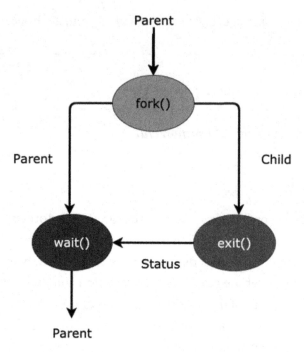

Figure 5-23. *Working mechanism of wait() system call*

Here's an example.

```c
#include<stdio.h>
#include<unistd.h>
#include<sys/wait.h>
 int main() {

   int status = fork();

   if (status == 0) {
       printf("Hello from child\n");
       printf("Child work is Completed and terminating.!\n");
   }else if(status > 0){
       printf("Hello from parent\n");
       wait(NULL);
       printf("Parent has terminated\n");
   }

   return 0;
}
```

In this program, the parent process is executed first, and then it enters a wait state. When the parent process enters a wait state, the child process enters the action to execute its assigned task. Once the child task is completed and terminated, the parent completes the remaining tasks that are assigned to it.

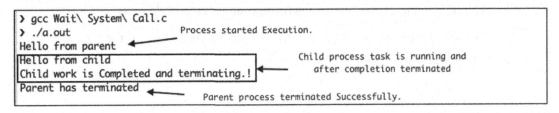

Figure 5-24. *Output of the C program for wait() system call*

waitpid System Call

The waitpid() system call is an advanced version of the wait() system call. It takes three parameters as arguments. The first parameter takes the child process identifier. The second parameter deals with the status of the child process and stores the status code of the child process. The third parameter is an options parameter that takes several options to get the child process-related information. The values that are passed to this argument are built-in macros. The return type of the waitpid system call is a process ID. If an error occurs, it returns –1.

The following shows the syntax.

pid_t waitpid(pid_t pid, int *status, int options)

The following are options parameters.

- WIFEXITED(status): It checks if the child exits normally or not.

- WEXITSTATUS(status): It returns the status code when a child exits.

- WIFSIGNALED(status): It informs the child exit status if the child exits because a signal was not caught.

- WTERMSIG(status): It gives the number of terminating signals.

- WIFSTOPPED(status): It returns the status information when the child stops execution.

- WSTOPSIG(status): It returns the number of stop signals in a program.

- WUNTRACED: It returns the child status that has stopped, but it doesn't trace the child.

- WNOHANG: It returns the status immediately if the child exits.

- WCONTINUED: It returns the status code if a signal resumes the stopped child process.

Here's an example.

```c
#include <stdio.h>
#include <unistd.h>
#include <sys/wait.h>

int main(){

    int pid;
    int status;

    pid = fork();

    // Terminates the Child process.
    if(!pid){
        printf("My PID: %d\n",getpid());
        _exit(0);
    }

    waitpid(pid,&status,WUNTRACED);

    if(WIFEXITED(status)) {
        printf("Exit Normally\n");
        printf("Exit status: %d\n",WEXITSTATUS(status));
        _exit(0);
    }else {
        printf("Exit NOT Normal\n");
        _exit(1);
    }
    return 0;
}
```

In this code, you get the status of the child process that is being terminated explicitly. WEXITSTATUS returns the status of the exited child process. WUNTRACED untraces the exited child process.

```
> gcc waitpid.c
> ./a.out
My PID: 27377  ◄━━━━━━  Child Process Id.
Exit Normally
Exit status: 0  ◄━━━━━━  Child Process Exit status.
```

Figure 5-25. *Output of C program using waitpid() system call*

kill System Call

A kill system call kills processes and signals. Killing a signal or process is the termination of a program/process/signal. The return type of this kill system call is an integer value. It returns 0 on the successful execution of the system call; otherwise, it returns –1 for an error.

The following shows the syntax.

int kill(pid_t pid, int sig);

- pid takes the process identifier of the process.

- sig takes the built-in signal parameter that needs to send to the process.

Here's an example.

```
#include<stdio.h>
#include<unistd.h>
#include<signal.h>

int main(){

    int pid = fork();

    if(pid == 0){
        printf("Child PID: %d\n",getpid());
```

```
    }else{
        printf("Parent PID: %d\n", getppid());
    }
    sleep(2);
    kill(getpid(), SIGQUIT);

    return 0;
}
```

This code prints the process ID of the child and parent processes. The current process ID is set to the kill system call that kills the currently running program after sleeping for two seconds.

```
> ./a.out
Parent PID: 7823
Child PID: 8005
[1]    8004 quit        ./a.out  ⟵———    Killing the process ./a.out
```

Figure 5-26. *Output of the C program for kill() system call*

exit System Call

An exit system call exits the calling process without executing the rest of the code that is present in the program. It is available in the stdlib.h library. The return of this system call is void. It doesn't return anything on execution.

The following shows the syntax.

void exit(int status)

status takes the value that is returned to the parent process.

Here's an example.

```
#include<stdio.h>
#include<stdlib.h>
#include<unistd.h>

int main(){

    int pid = fork();
```

```
if(pid == 0){
    // Prints the Child Process ID.
    printf("Child Process ID: %d\n", getpid());
    exit(0);
}else{
    // Prints the Parent Process ID.
    printf("Parent Process Id: %d\n", getppid());
    exit(0);
}

printf("Processes are exited and this line will not print\n");

return 0;
}
```

This code prints the parent and child process ID and exits the program without executing the last printf statement. This is because the exit() system call has exited the parent and child processes, and there is no process left to execute the last printf statement, so it doesn't print to the console screen.

```
> gcc exit.c
> ./a.out
Parent Process Id: 3324  ◄─────  Process Id of the Parent Process.
Child Process ID: 3399   ◄─────  Process Id of the Child Process.
```

Figure 5-27. *Output of the C program for exit() system call*

_Exit System Call

_Exit terminates the process normally, but it doesn't perform any cleanup activity. This system call is available in the unistd.h library. The return type of this system call is void. It doesn't return anything. After the process is terminated, the control is given to the host environment (currently running) in this system call.

The following shows the syntax.

void _Exit(int status)

status takes the value, which is returned to the parent process.

Here's an example.

```
#include<stdio.h>
#include<stdlib.h>
#include<unistd.h>

int main(){

    printf("Current Running Process ID: %d\n", getpid());
    _Exit(0);
    printf("Nothing will execute\n");
    return 0;
}
```

This code does not give any results. It simply terminates the process and returns control to the host environment.

Introduction to Signals

A signal is a software interrupt or an event generated by a Unix/Linux system in response to a condition or an action. There are several signals available in the Unix system. All signal mechanisms are implemented in the signals.h library. In this section, the signals.h library is used to create custom signals and to handle the signals that are created by the system. When a signal is raised, the kernel is guided as discussed next.

Catch the Signal

When the kernel raises a signal, you can create a custom routine to handle the signal. But to use your custom handling routines, the process needs to register the custom routine before the processed signal is delivered to the user space.

Ignore the Signal

When the program is raising a signal, and that signal has no effect, you go to the ignore case. This ignores the signal that does not affect the program, but you need to explicitly mention it before the signal is delivered. All signals can't be ignored. The signals that have no effect on raising a signal can be ignored.

Default Action

When a program raises a signal, and that signal is neither caught nor ignored, it is handled by the default built-in signal handler that is defined by the system. It is an implicit system behavior meant for handling the signal. But a process can explicitly request to use the built-in signal handler in the program. Default handlers do not always terminate a process.

Every signal has certain attributes. The name and the signal number identify the signal very easily. Every signal has a certain functionality associated with it, which makes signals very handy. All the available built-in signals supported by the system can be printed with the kill command.

```
kill -1
```

The signals in Figure 5-28 are the signals that are supported by the Linux system.

```
srimani@srimani-crypter:~$ kill -1
 1) SIGHUP       2) SIGINT       3) SIGQUIT      4) SIGILL       5) SIGTRAP
 6) SIGABRT      7) SIGBUS       8) SIGFPE       9) SIGKILL     10) SIGUSR1
11) SIGSEGV     12) SIGUSR2     13) SIGPIPE     14) SIGALRM     15) SIGTERM
16) SIGSTKFLT   17) SIGCHLD     18) SIGCONT     19) SIGSTOP     20) SIGTSTP
21) SIGTTIN     22) SIGTTOU     23) SIGURG      24) SIGXCPU     25) SIGXFSZ
26) SIGVTALRM   27) SIGPROF     28) SIGWINCH    29) SIGIO       30) SIGPWR
31) SIGSYS      34) SIGRTMIN    35) SIGRTMIN+1  36) SIGRTMIN+2  37) SIGRTMIN+3
38) SIGRTMIN+4  39) SIGRTMIN+5  40) SIGRTMIN+6  41) SIGRTMIN+7  42) SIGRTMIN+8
43) SIGRTMIN+9  44) SIGRTMIN+10 45) SIGRTMIN+11 46) SIGRTMIN+12 47) SIGRTMIN+13
48) SIGRTMIN+14 49) SIGRTMIN+15 50) SIGRTMAX-14 51) SIGRTMAX-13 52) SIGRTMAX-12
53) SIGRTMAX-11 54) SIGRTMAX-10 55) SIGRTMAX-9  56) SIGRTMAX-8  57) SIGRTMAX-7
58) SIGRTMAX-6  59) SIGRTMAX-5  60) SIGRTMAX-4  61) SIGRTMAX-3  62) SIGRTMAX-2
63) SIGRTMAX-1  64) SIGRTMAX
```

Figure 5-28. *List of all the built-in signals*

The commonly used signals and the functionalities are described in Table 5-2.

Table 5-2. *Signals and Their Functionality*

Signal Name	Signal Number	Signal Functionality
SIGHUP	1	Hang up a signal
SIGINT	2	Interrupt (Ctrl+C)
SIGQUIT	3	Quit (Ctrl+D)
SIGABRT	6	Process Abort
SIGKILL	9	Kills the process without cleanup activity
SIGUSR1	10	User-defined signal 1
SIGSEGV	11	Invalid Memory Segment Access
SIGUSR2	12	User-defined signal 2
SIGALRM	14	Alarm Signal
SIGTERM	15	Program/Software Termination Signal
SIGCHLD	17	Child process has stopped or exited
SIGCONT	18	Continue Execution
SIGSTOP	19	Stop Execution
SIGTSTP	20	Stop Signal
SIGTTIN	21	Background process trying to read
SIGTTOU	22	Background process trying to write

The actual list of signals may vary between Solaris and Linux. All the signal lists are available in the signal.h library. By using signals, you can set traps and interrupts. In the C standard library, there is a signal() system call that creates the signals. The return type of the signal system call is a pointer to a function that takes the single integer parameter and returns nothing (i.e., void). If successful, this system call returns the previous action. If any error occurs, it returns SIG_ERR to indicate the error. This system call also has a typedef version that is easy to read and understand. But in this chapter, you are dealing with the syntax of the original signal system call.

CHAPTER 5 PROCESS AND SIGNALS

The following shows the syntax.

void (*signal(int sig, void (*function)(int)))(int)

- sig takes the signal number. The signal number completely depends on the purpose and the type of signal you want to send.

- function is a pointer that points to either the function implemented by the programmer or the built-in ones. These are the built-in functions.

  - SIG_DFL handles the signal by default. It is considered the default handling of signals, which means it sends the interrupt that is caused by the program.

  - SIG_IGN ignores the signal that is caused by the program.

Here's an example.

```
#include <stdio.h>
#include <unistd.h>
#include <stdlib.h>
#include <signal.h>

void CUSTOM_HANDLER(int);

int main () {

   // SIGINT is used to intimate when any interrupt occurs to
   // the program.
   signal(SIGINT, CUSTOM_HANDLER);

   while(1) {
      printf("Hello World...!\n");
      sleep(1);
   }

   return 0;
}

// This function will call when any signal interrupt occurs.
```

```
void CUSTOM_HANDLER(int signum) {
  printf("Caught signal %d, coming out from Program\n", signum);
  exit(1);
}
```

This code prints "Hello World…!" an infinite number of times. If an interrupt occurs in the program, SIGINT immediately catches that signal and sends it to the CUSTOM_HANDLER function to handle it.

```
> gcc Signal\ Generation\ and\ Handling.c
> ./a.out
Hello World...!
Hello World...!
Hello World...!
Hello World...!
^C
Caught signal 2, coming out from Program  ◄─────    Interrupt Signal Caught
                                                    and Handled by the
                                                    custom Handler.
```

Figure 5-29. *Signal generation output*

Types of Signals

In Unix/Linux, signals are classified into two types based on functionality: unreliable and reliable.

Unreliable Signals

Signals that doesn't have any available installed signal handler and become lost means the process never knows about the signal that is being raised by the system. A process has very little control over unreliable signals. The process can catch a signal or ignore it, but blocking a signal is not possible with unreliable signals. A *blocking operation* means intimating the operating system explicitly to hold the signal for a certain time and releasing it when asked by the program.

Reliable Signals

Signals that are not lost in the system are reliable. The process has complete control and can catch, ignore, and block signals using system calls. These signals are the enhanced version in Unix-based system.

System Calls for Signals

There are different system calls available in the signal.h library that manipulates the signals. Signal manipulation can be done with the following system calls.

- raise

- kill

- alarm

- pause

- abort

- sleep

raise System Call

A raise system call raises a signal by the process itself. The return type of this system call is an integer. This system call returns zero on success and nonzero if a failure occurs.

The following shows the syntax.

int raise(int sig)

sig is the signal number that needs to be sent. This parameter depends on the type of signal you want to raise explicitly to the process itself. The signal numbers are from the built-in signals list.

Here's an example.

```
#include <stdio.h>
#include<stdlib.h>
#include <signal.h>

void SIGNAL_HANDLER(int);

int main () {

    signal(SIGINT, SIGNAL_HANDLER);
    printf("Raising a new signal\n");
    int status = raise(SIGINT);
```

```
  if(status != 0){
    printf("Something went wrong Unable to raise the new signal\n");
  }

  return 0;
}

void SIGNAL_HANDLER(int signal) {
  printf("signal caught and handled gracefully\n");
}
```

This code raises a signal for the running process, and that signal is handled by SIGNAL_HANDLER.

```
> gcc raise.c
> ./a.out
Raising a new signal  ◄─────── Raising a new signal.
signal caught and handled gracefully ◄─────── Raised signal got handled.
```

Figure 5-30.   *Output of the raise system call*

kill System Call

A kill system call sends signals to other processes as well itself. A kill system call can also kill processes. The killing/terminating of a signal is similar to killing/terminating a process in an operating system.

alarm System Call

In signals, there is an alarm clock facility that schedules the signal trap for the future. This system call is used by the process to schedule the SIG_ALARM signal. The return type of the alarm system call is an unsigned integer. It returns the number of seconds remaining in the set time that is to be delivered. If no alarm is set, it returns 0.

The following shows the syntax.

unsigned int alarm(unsigned int seconds)

seconds takes time in the form of seconds. The second's value must be a positive number.

Here's an example.

```
#include<stdio.h>
#include<stdlib.h>
#include<unistd.h>
#include<signal.h>

void raisedAlarm(int sig);

int main(){

    alarm(5);

    signal(SIGALRM, raisedAlarm);

    while(1){
        printf("Hello World...!\n");
        sleep(1);
    }

    return 0;
}
void raisedAlarm(int sig){
    printf("The Alarm has Raised.\n");
    exit(0);
}
```

This code raises the alarm after seconds of code execution. It is very handy to set signal traps for time-dependent applications. Since the exit() function is used in the raisedAlarm function, it terminates the program.

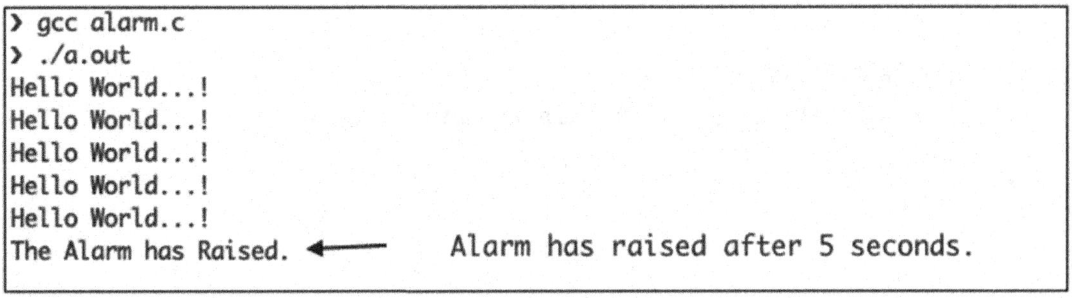

```
> gcc alarm.c
> ./a.out
Hello World...!
Hello World...!
Hello World...!
Hello World...!
Hello World...!
The Alarm has Raised. ◄────    Alarm has raised after 5 seconds.
```

Figure 5-31. *Output of the alarm system call*

159

pause System Call

The pause system call suspends the execution of a program until a signal occurs. The return type of a pause system call is an integer. It takes 0 parameters. It returns –1 on failure; otherwise, it returns the respective signal catching function.

The following shows the syntax.

int pause(void)

Here's an example.

```
#include <stdio.h>
#include <unistd.h>
#include <stdlib.h>
#include <signal.h>

void SIGNAL_HANDLER(int);

int main(void){

    alarm(10);

    signal(SIGALRM, SIGNAL_HANDLER);

    if(alarm(7) > 0){
        printf("An alarm has been set already.\n");
    }

    pause();

    printf("You will not see this text.\n");

    return 1;
}

void SIGNAL_HANDLER(int signo){
    printf("Caught the signal with number: %d\n", signo);
    exit(0);
}
```

This code catches the alarm signal interrupt. The remaining code below pause() does not work. This is because pause() suspends the current running program, but the alarm function and its handlers work parallelly. When SIGALRM is raised, the custom handler handles it.

```
> gcc pause.c
> ./a.out
An alarm has been set already. ◄──────── Alarm is set for 10 sec.
Caught the signal with number: 14 ◄── This signal handler will
                                      caught after 10 sec.
```

Figure 5-32. *Output of pause system call*

abort System Call

The abort system call terminates the program or process abnormally. This system call returns a void type. It takes zero parameters. This system call sends the SIGABRT signal to the process to terminate. This signal is not able to be overridden by other signals. This system call does not close all the files and pointers opened by the process since it causes an abnormal termination of the program.

The following shows the syntax.

void abort(void)

Here's an example.

```
#include<stdio.h>
#include<unistd.h>
#include<stdlib.h>
#include<signal.h>

int main(){

    int status = fork();

    if(status == 0){
        printf("Child Process ID: %d\n", getpid());
    }else if(status > 0){
        printf("Parent Process ID: %d\n", getpid());
    }
```

```
    abort();
    printf("Due to abnormal termination this line will not execute.\n");

    return 0;
}
```

This program creates a child and parent process. After creating processes, the remaining lines of code that are present below abort() are not executed. This is because abort terminates the program abnormally. But the output of the program may differ.

```
> gcc abort.c
> ./a.out
Parent Process ID: 1376   ◄────────   Parent Process Id.
[1]    1376 abort      ./a.out  ◄────────   Aborted the program.
Child Process ID: 1377  ◄────────        Child process Id.
```

Figure 5-33.   *Output of the abort system call*

sleep System Call

This sleep system call sleeps the thread until the specified number of seconds have elapsed or a signal hits (which is not ignored). The return type of this system call is an unsigned integer. It returns 0 if the requested time has elapsed, or the number of seconds left to sleep if the call is interrupted by a signal handler.

The following shows the syntax.

unsigned int sleep(unsigned int seconds)

seconds takes the number of seconds that the process or thread wants to sleep as an argument.

Here's an example.

```
#include<stdio.h>
#include<unistd.h>
#include<stdlib.h>
```

```
int main(){

    for(int i=0; i<5; i++){
        printf("Hello World.\n");
        sleep(1);
    }

    return 0;
}
```

This code prints "Hello World" five times by sleeping for 1 second after every iteration of the loop.

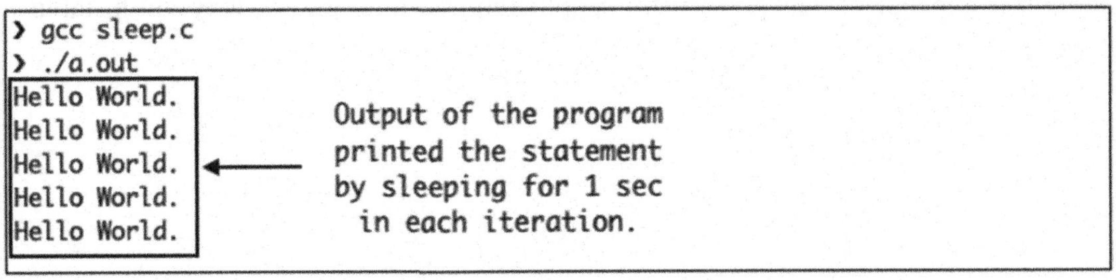

```
> gcc sleep.c
> ./a.out
Hello World.
Hello World.        Output of the program
Hello World.   ◄─   printed the statement
Hello World.        by sleeping for 1 sec
Hello World.           in each iteration.
```

Figure 5-34. *Output of sleep system call*

Summary

In this chapter, you were introduced to the process environment, including how to create and terminate a process.

- You looked at the environment variable and how to create it programmatically and by using commands.

- You explored the memory layout of the C program and how things are stored in a computer's memory.

- Kernel support for the process teaches you about the Linux subsystem. In the Linux subsystem, you looked at various management schemes done by the Linux kernel internally.

- The creation of processes achieves concurrency. You learned a lot about how to create processes using built-in system calls in C.

- You learned that a process could become a zombie or an orphan.

- You learned about the various system calls that are available for process management. The system calls include vfork(), wait(), waitpid(), kill(), execv family system calls, and exit(), and _Exit() system calls.

- You saw signals and traps set in a program to create your custom interrupt in a program. You learned types of signals and system calls for signal management include abort(), sleep(), pause(), alarm(), raise(), and kill().

You now know the core concepts of process and signals in an operating system. You should be able to work with your custom applications and scripts in a very comfortable manner.

CHAPTER 6

Interprocess Communication

Interprocess communication (IPC) is a mechanism that is widely used in an operating system to effectively access shared data. This mechanism is very important to the design process of microkernel and nanokernel development. An IPC mechanism is usually seen in a distributed computing environment, but it is also widely used in traditional computing environments. There are two types of IPC mechanisms: synchronous and asynchronous. In this chapter, you learn about the various techniques that achieve IPC. The following topics are covered.

- Introduction to IPC

- Benefits of IPC

- Modes of transmission

- Types of IPC

- Anonymous pipes

- APIs for anonymous pipes

- Implementation of anonymous pipes

- Named pipes, or FIFO

- Implementation of FIFO

- Introduction to message queues

- APIs for message queues

- Implementation of message queues

- Introduction to semaphores

© Sri Manikanta Palakollu 2021
S. M. Palakollu, *Practical System Programming with C*, https://doi.org/10.1007/978-1-4842-6321-1_6

- Characteristics of semaphores

- Advantages and disadvantages of semaphores

- APIs for semaphores

- Race condition examples

- Solving the race condition by using semaphore and mutex mechanisms

Introduction to IPC

Interprocess communication is a mechanism that lets processes communicate with other processes in an operating system. The process can be in the same system or a different system. IPC also involves synchronizing the actions of processes and managing data-sharing activity. The processes in an operating system are of two types: independent and cooperating.

Independent Processes

A process that doesn't share data with other processes is an *independent process*. It doesn't affect other processes, and it is not affected by other processes. Independent processes are not involved in any interprocess communication activity.

Cooperating Processes

A process that shares data with other processes is called a *cooperating process*. These processes achieve interprocess communication in an operating system. A cooperating process helps you achieve IPC in a system. Interprocess communication between processes are achieved in two ways: shared memory and message passing.

Shared Memory

The IPC methodology simultaneously gives common memory access to multiple processes. It helps multiple processes communicate with each other. All POSIX-based and Windows operating systems use a shared memory mechanism to perform IPC.

Message Passing

Message passing is a model for performing IPC in an operating system. It is done by reading and writing data to the message queue created using the msgget() system call without being connected. Messages are stored in a queue until the receiver retrieves it.

Message passing helps you achieve different modes of communication.

- Communication between different threads within a process.

- Communication between different processes running on the same host machine.

- Communication between different processes running on different machines.

IPC Between Processes

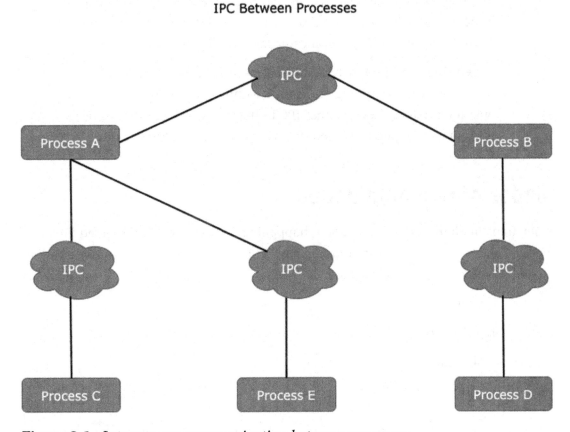

Figure 6-1. *Interprocess communication between processes*

In Figure 6-1, there are five processes. Let's assume for now that all the processes belong to the same operating system, and some processes want to communicate with each other to share data and perform a system or user activity. IPC comes into the picture. It achieves communication between multiple processes. In this OS example, process A wants to share data with process C and process E. This is done with IPC.

The Benefits of IPC

The following are some of the benefits of IPC.

- **Information sharing:** Sharing common information between processes is easy and offers better communication.

- **Modularity:** Modularity divides large code into smaller chunks. This modular code executes simultaneously on the system. Development is made easy with modularity. (But debugging becomes harder when several processes are communicating with each other.)

- **Speed:** A large task/activity is broken into smaller subtasks. Each subtask is assigned to separate threads within a process in the operating system. Processes use IPC to share data and improve computational speed by executing multiple tasks simultaneously.

Modes of Communication

When transmission or communication is happening between two parties, it requires a medium and mode of transfer to communicate. There are three types of communication modes available for communication.

- Simplex
- Half Duplex
- Full Duplex

Simplex

In a *simplex mode* of data transmission, data is transferred in a unidirectional way, which means that only one process, one person, or one device can send data that others receive. Real examples of a simplex data mode transmission are radio and television broadcasting. The scope of this book focuses on unidirectional data transmission between processes.

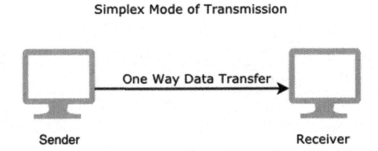

Simplex Mode of Transmission

One Way Data Transfer

Sender   Receiver

Figure 6-2. *Simplex mode of data transmission*

Half Duplex

In a *half-duplex mode* of data transmission, data is transmitted bidirectionally but not at the same time. In this mechanism, a process, or a person, or a device has access to send and receive data but not at the same time. When one process is sending, the other processes must listen or receive. The best example of a half-duplex mode of data transmission is a walkie-talkie. This type of communication mechanism is used when there is no need for bidirectional communication at the same time.

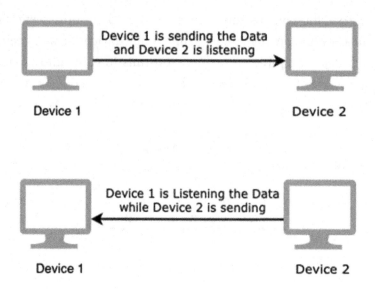

Figure 6-3. *Half-duplex mode of data transmission*

Full Duplex

In a *full-duplex mode* of data transmission, data is transferred in a bidirectional way between two processes, or two persons, or two devices. This mode of transmission is used when bidirectional communication is needed between processes. The best example of a full-duplex mode of data transmission is a telephone, in which two people can speak simultaneously.

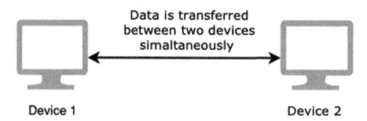

Figure 6-4. *Full-duplex mode of data transmission*

Types of IPC

Interprocess communication establishes communication between different processes. This communication is done in two ways.

- Communication between two related processes (i.e., child and parent processes). Figure 6-5 represents IPC between different processes on a same machine using a single kernel.

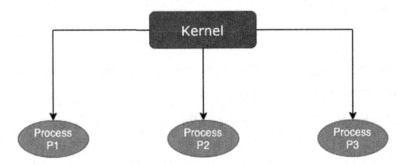

Figure 6-5. *Communication between related processes*

- Communication between unrelated processes (i.e., two or more processes other than parent and child processes). Figure 6-6 represents IPC between different processes on different systems.

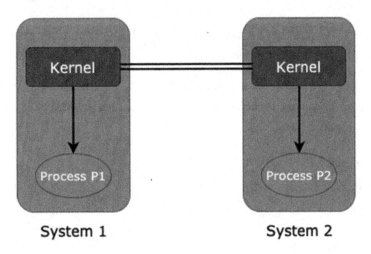

Figure 6-6. *Communication between unrelated processes*

171

The available mechanisms that achieve IPC in operating systems are discussed next.

Pipes

A pipe establishes a connection between two related processes.

- Pipes are classified into two types.

    - Named/FIFO pipes

    - Unnamed/anonymous pipes

- Pipes follow a unidirectional (half-duplex) mechanism to establish communication between processes.

- A pipe has two file descriptors: one for reading and the other for writing.

Figure 6-7. *The architecture of an anonymous pipe*

- Figure 6-7 shows that a pipe can write/send data from one side and the other side can read/receive it.

- To achieve a full-duplex mechanism in pipes, you need to use two pipes: one pipe reads the data from the pipe, and the other one writes the data to the pipe.

- The operations that use pipes are write and read operations.

- A pipe creates using a pipe() system call.

FIFO (Named Pipe)

FIFO (*first in, first out*) establishes a connection between two unrelated processes.

- FIFO is also called a *named pipe*.

- FIFO is an extension of the traditional pipe in the Unix system.

- FIFO uses the unidirectional (half-duplex) mechanism to establish communication between processes.

- A named pipe is created using the mkfifo() system call.

Message Queues

Message queues establish communication between multiple processes using a full-duplex mechanism.

- It uses the asynchronous mechanism to serve the processes.

- The operating system's kernel manages message queues.

- It is an easy way to transfer the data between processes.

- A message queue is created using a msgget() system call that returns the queue identifier.

Semaphores

A semaphore provides synchronization of the data to avoid race conditions.

- When two or more processes are accessing the same code/data block in a program, the block is called the *critical section*.

- A *race condition* is a situation that occurs inside a critical section when two or more threads are trying to access and change the same data at the same time. This leads to incorrect results. Synchronization is required to avoid this situation. It is done with semaphores and other locking mechanisms.

- A semaphore maintains data consistency and security. Data consistency refers to the maintenance of data without any loss, even when multiple threads and processes are using it.

Shared Memory

Shared memory communicates between multiple processes using common shared memory.

Shared memory needs to be protected from race conditions. This is done by using a semaphore technique. Race conditions can also be avoided using proper thread synchronization techniques and locking mechanisms.

Sockets

Sockets establish communication over a network.

- IPC between different computers is achieved using the socket mechanism.

- It enables you to use channel-based communication over a network.

- Data is transferred based on protocol standards.

- In the TCP protocol standard, data is transferred in sequential order.

- There is no standard for data transfer in the UDP protocol.

Anonymous Pipes

Anonymous pipes create a communication medium between interrelated processes. Anonymous pipes are also called *unnamed pipes*. Anonymous pipes establish a communication parent process and child process or a parent process and grandchild process. The working mechanism of a pipe is represented in Figure 6-8.

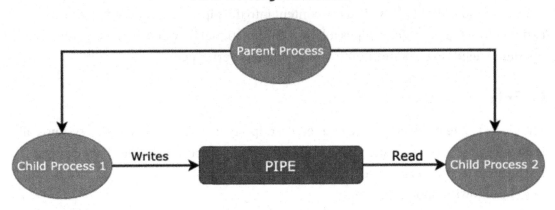

PIPE Working Mechanism

Figure 6-8. *Anonymous pipe working mechanism*

When process1 writes data to the pipe, it is read by another process using a file descriptor. When data is written to the main memory, the pipe treats that data as a virtual file. Accessing that data is done with a file descriptor. The write and read operations in files are done with two standard file descriptors. The most common example of a pipe is a shell command using a pipe symbol.

APIs for Anonymous Pipes

Anonymous pipes are created with the help of pipe() system call available in <unistd.h> library since they are part of the traditional Unix system. The system calls that perform IPC using traditional Unix pipes are pipe(), write(), read(), and close(). The syntax and working principles of these system calls are discussed next.

pipe()

The pipe() system call opens the file descriptors that communicate with different Linux processes. This system call creates a pipe that transmits the data in a unidirectional way to establish an IPC between the related processes. It creates two file descriptors: one for reading and the for writing. The return type of this system call is an integer. It returns 0 if successful; if it fails, it returns –1 with a respective error code. The error code is obtained with the perror() system call.

The following shows the syntax.

```
int pipe(int pipefd[2])
```

pipefd takes an integer descriptor array of size 2, which performs the read and write operations. Pipefd[1] writes the content into the pipe, and pipefd[0] reads the content from the pipe. Since pipes follow a unidirectional flow of data transfer, the read operation needs to be done after the write action is performed.

close()

The close() system call closes the opened descriptors. The return type of this system call is an integer. It returns 0 if successful and –1 if any failure occurs. When you want to get the error code, you need to use the perror() system call.

The following shows the syntax.

int close(int fd)

fd takes the file descriptor parameter and closes the given file descriptor. Once a file descriptor is closed, it is no longer available to use again.

write()

The write() system call writes the content to a specific file with certain arguments of that file descriptor. This system call uses a buffer to write the content into the file descriptor. The return type of this system call is ssize_t. If successful, it returns the number of bytes written to the file; otherwise, it returns –1.

The following shows the syntax.

ssize_t write(int fd, const void *buf, size_t count)

- fd takes the file descriptor that is created with the pipe() system call to uniquely identify the file descriptor.

- buf takes the message that is written to the pipe or file descriptor.

- count takes the size of the buffer that is writing to the pipe/file descriptor.

read()

The read() system call reads the content from the file descriptor or pipe. The return type of this system call is ssize_t. It returns the number of bytes read from the file descriptor and returns –1 if any failure occurs.

The following shows the syntax.

`ssize_t read(int fd, void *buf, size_t count)`

- fd takes the file descriptor that is created using a pipe() system call to uniquely identify the descriptor.

- buf is the buffer value that reads the message from the file descriptor or pipe.

- count takes the size of the buffer that is reading from the descriptor/pipe.

Creating Anonymous Pipes

This section deals with the creation of traditional Unix pipes to perform interprocess communication using file descriptors. A pipe's flow of construction is represented using a flowchart shown in Figure 6-9. The following steps achieve IPC using pipes.

1. Create a pipe using the pipe() system call.

2. If the user quits, the program terminates; otherwise, go to step 3.

3. Write the data into the pipe using a write() system call.

4. Once the write operation is done, the read() system call reads the data from the pipe.

5. Steps 3 and 4 repeat until the user quits the program.

Flow Chart of Anonymous Pipes

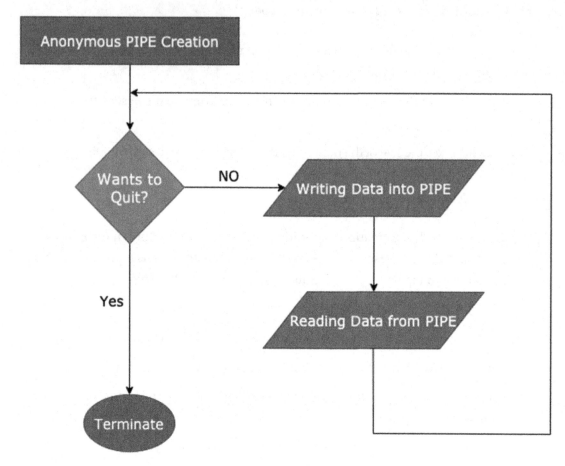

Figure 6-9. *Flowchart of an anonymous pipe*

The following is an example.

```
#include<stdio.h>
#include<string.h>
#include<unistd.h>

#define BUFFER_SIZE 1024

// Global Variables
int pipefds[2];
int status;
char writemessage[BUFFER_SIZE];
```

```c
char readmessage[BUFFER_SIZE];

// pipeOperation() to perform read and write Operations.
void pipeOperation(){
  printf("Writing to pipe - Message is %s", writemessage);
  write(pipefds[1], writemessage, sizeof(writemessage));
  read(pipefds[0], readmessage, sizeof(readmessage));
  printf("Reading from pipe - Message is %s", readmessage);
}
int main() {

  status = pipe(pipefds);
  if (status == -1) {
    printf("Unable to create pipe\n");
    return 1;
  }

  printf("Enter the message to write into Pipe\n");
  printf("To exit type \"quit\" \n");

  fgets(writemessage, BUFSIZ, stdin);
// This loop is used to take continuous Standard input.
  while (strcmp(writemessage, "quit\n") != 0) {
      pipeOperation();
      fgets(writemessage, BUFSIZ, stdin);
   }

  close(pipefds[0]);
  close(pipefds[1]);

  return 0;
}
```

Figure 6-10 shows the output.

```
> gcc pipes.c -o pipe  ◄─────────────────── Compiling the Code.
> ./pipe
Enter the message to write into Pipe
To exit type "quit"
Hello World....!
Writing to pipe - Message is Hello World....!
Reading from pipe — Message is Hello World....!
Hey
Writing to pipe - Message is Hey                    Writing the Content
Reading from pipe — Message is Hey    ◄──────────      to the pipe and
Hi                                                  reading it from the pipe.
Writing to pipe - Message is Hi
Reading from pipe — Message is Hi
Practical System programming with c.
Writing to pipe - Message is Practical System programming with c.
Reading from pipe — Message is Practical System programming with c.
quit
```

Figure 6-10. *The output of the anonymous pipe program*

Implementation of Pipes Using Child and Parent Processes

This section creates pipes and performs read and write operations using child and parent processes. The flow of pipe construction and the operations of a pipe are represented in a flowchart in Figure 6-11. The following steps handle the operation of a pipe.

1. Create a pipe using the pipe() system call.

2. If the user quits, the program terminates; otherwise, create a child process.

3. Write the data into the pipe using the parent process.

4. Read the data from the pipe using the child process.

5. Steps 3 and 4 repeat until the user quits.

Handling the PIPES Using Child and Parent Processes

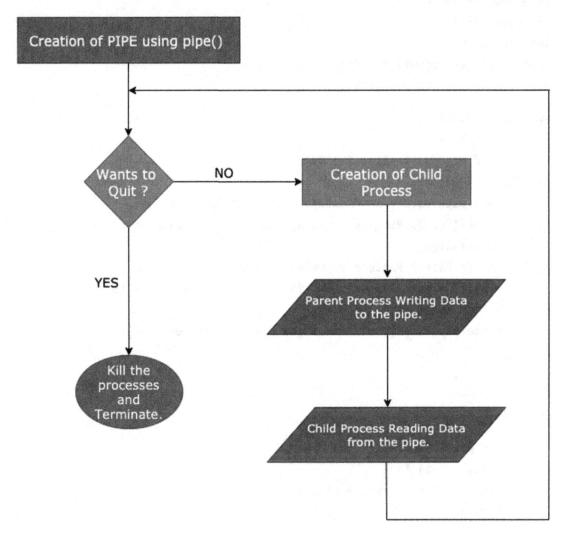

Figure 6-11. *Flow chart of anonymous pipes handling through child and parent processes*

The following is an example.

```
#include<stdio.h>
#include<string.h>
#include<unistd.h>
#include<signal.h>
```

```
#define BUFFER_SIZE 1024

// Global Variables
int pipefds[2];
int status, pid;
char writemessage[BUFFER_SIZE];
char readmessage[BUFFER_SIZE];

void pipeOperation(){
   pid = fork();
   // Child Process to Read the Data.
   if(pid == 0){
      read(pipefds[0], readmessage, sizeof(readmessage));
      printf("Child Process: Reading from pipe - Message is %s",
      readmessage);
   }else{   // Parent Process to write the data.
      printf("Parent Process: Writing to pipe - Message is %s",
      writemessage);
      write(pipefds[1], writemessage, sizeof(writemessage));
   }

}

int main() {

  status = pipe(pipefds);
  if (status == -1) {
    printf("Unable to create pipe\n");
    return 1;
  }

  printf("Enter the message to write into Pipe\n");
  printf("To exit type \"quit\" \n");

  fgets(writemessage, BUFSIZ, stdin);

  while (strcmp(writemessage, "quit\n") != 0) {
      pipeOperation();
      fgets(writemessage, BUFSIZ, stdin);
```

```
        kill(pid, SIGKILL); // Killing
    }

  return 0;
}
```

Figure 6-12 shows the output.

```
> gcc pipes_with_processes.c -o pipeoperations  ◄─────────    Compiling the Code.
> ./pipeoperations
Enter the message to write into Pipe
To exit type "quit"
Hello
Parent Process: Writing to pipe - Message is Hello
Child Process: Reading from pipe — Message is Hello
Practical System Programming with C.                         Parent Process is used to
Parent Process: Writing to pipe - Message is Practical System Programming with C.    write the data into
Child Process: Reading from pipe — Message is Practical System Programming with C. ◄──── pipe and Child process is
Java Programming                                             used to read the data
Parent Process: Writing to pipe - Message is Java Programming    from the pipe.
Child Process: Reading from pipe — Message is Java Programming
Joshua Caled
Parent Process: Writing to pipe - Message is Joshua Caled
Child Process: Reading from pipe — Message is Joshua Caled
quit
```

Figure 6-12. *The output of the anonymous pipes handled by child and parent processes*

Working with Named Pipes

Named pipes (also called FIFO) communicate with two unrelated processes. Traditional Unix pipes achieve IPC between related processes. When you want to communicate with an unrelated/different process, then FIFO achieves it. A named pipe is used for bidirectional communication. In traditional Unix pipes, bidirectional communication is done with two different pipes: one for writing the data and the other for reading the data. A named pipe can be created with two different system calls: mknod() or mkfifo().

mknod() System Call

The mknod system call creates a special file, device file, or FIFO file. This system call is available in a sys/stat.h header file. The return type of this system call is an integer. On the successful execution of a system call, it returns 0; if any error occurs, it returns –1.

The following shows the syntax.

`int mknod(const char *pathname, mode_t mode, dev_t dev)`

- `pathname` takes the complete path of the creating FIFO, or device file, or ordinary file to where you want to place that file in your system memory. The pathname is relative; if you don't specify the path, then it is created in the program execution current directory.

- `mode` represents the type of file. The available file types are shown in Table 6-1.

Table 6-1. *Available File Types*

File Type	Description
S_IFIFO	FIFO Special
S_IFCHR	Character Special
S_IFREG	Regular File
S_IFDIR	Directory
S_IFLNK	Symbolic Link
S_IFBLK	Block Special File

None of the file types are portable except S_IFIFO.

Dev

Dev represents the permissions that you can assign to a newly created file. The available file permissions are described in Table 6-2.

Table 6-2. *Available File Permissions*

File Mode	Description
S_IRWXU	Read, write, and execute permissions by the owner
S_IRUSR	Read permissions by the owner
S_IWUSR	Write permissions by the owner
S_IXUSR	Execute permissions by the owner
S_IRWXG	Read, write, execute permissions by group
S_IRGRP	Read permission by group
S_IWGRP	Write permissions by group
S_IXGRP	Execute permissions by group
S_IRWXO	Read, write, execute permissions by others
S_IROTH	Read permissions by others
S_IWOTH	Write permissions by others
S_IXOTH	Execute permissions by others

You can also give permissions to a file using the octal representation, as explained in Chapter 1.

mkfifo() System Call

The mkfifo system call creates the FIFO special file. This system call is available in the sys/stat.h library. The return type of this system call is an integer. It returns 0 on the successful creation of a FIFO special file. If any error occurs, then it returns –1, and no FIFO is created.

The following shows the syntax.

int mkfifo(const char *pathname, mode_t mode)

- **pathname** takes the path of the special FIFO file. The path may be relative or absolute. If the path is not specified, it is created in the current program's executing directory.

- **mode** represents the permission that you want to keep for the newly created FIFO file. All the file mode permissions are the same as the mknod's system call.

mknod vs. mkfifo

Both system calls create a FIFO special file. The mkfifo system call can create a standard and portable FIFO, whereas mknod can't create a standard and portable FIFO. The mknod system call creates not only FIFO but also different types of files. It is highly recommended that you use mkfifo to create a FIFO for IPC because it makes communication more reliable than mknod.

Creating FIFO

This section creates a simple communication application that sends data from the client to the server using named pipes. The server reads the content that is sent by the client. The client sends the data to the server. The server has read permissions, whereas the client has write permissions.

Let's look at the server and client working mechanisms.

FIFO Server

A FIFO server reads the data sent by the client using the named pipe that establishes an IPC between the processes. The workflow of the FIFO server is represented as a flowchart in Figure 6-13. The following are the steps involved in a FIFO server.

1. Create a named pipe using mkfifo().

2. Open the named pipe with read-only permissions.

3. Accept the messages/data from the FIFO client.

4. If the client sends a quit message, it prints on the standard console and terminates the server program.

5. If the client sends a normal message, it prints it to the standard console and waits to receive messages from the client.

6. Step 5 repeats until the client quits the server program.

Working Mechanism of FIFO Server

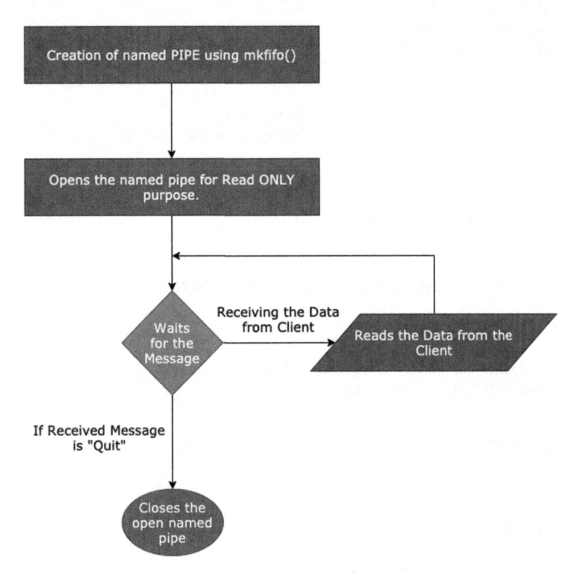

Figure 6-13. *FIFO server working mechanism architecture*

```
#include <stdio.h>
#include <unistd.h>
#include <string.h>
#include <sys/stat.h>
#include <sys/types.h>
#include <fcntl.h>
```

```
#define FIFO_FILE "FIFO"
int file_descriptor;
char message_buffer[1024];
int read_buffer_bytes;
void receiveData(){
  while(1) {
      file_descriptor = open(FIFO_FILE, O_RDONLY);
      read_buffer_bytes = read(file_descriptor, message_buffer,
      sizeof(message_buffer));
      message_buffer[read_buffer_bytes] = '\0';
      if((int)strlen(message_buffer) == 0){
         close(file_descriptor);
         break;
      }
      printf("Received Message: %s\n", message_buffer);
  }
}
int main() {
  // Create the FIFO if it does not exist
  mknod(FIFO_FILE, S_IFIFO|0640, 0);

  // Function to receive the data from pipe.
  receiveData();

  return 0;
}
```

FIFO Client

A FIFO client sends data to the server using named pipes. The overall workflow of a FIFO client is represented as a flowchart in Figure 6-14. The following steps are used by the FIFO client.

1. Create a named pipe using mkfifo().

2. Open the named pipe with write-only permissions.

3. Wait for the message from the client.

4. If the message is to quit, then the client and server immediately quit and print the quit message.

5. If the client enters any other message, it is sent to the server. The server receives the message and prints it to the screen. During this process, IPC takes place between the processes.

6. Step 5 repeats until the client quits the program.

Working Mechanism of FIFO Client

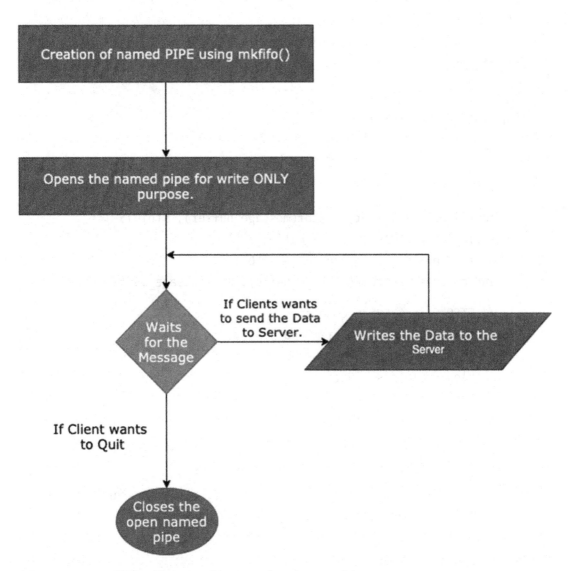

Figure 6-14. *FIFO client working mechanism architecture*

```c
#include <stdio.h>
#include<stdlib.h>
#include <unistd.h>
#include <string.h>
#include <sys/stat.h>
#include <sys/types.h>
#include <fcntl.h>

#define FIFO_FILE "FIFO"

// Global Variables Data
int file_descriptor;
int end_process;
int stringlen;
char message_buffer[1024];
char end_message_buffer[5];

void sendMessage(){

  while (1) {

        fgets(message_buffer, sizeof(message_buffer), stdin);
        stringlen = strlen(message_buffer);
        message_buffer[stringlen - 1] = '\0';
        end_process = strcmp(message_buffer, end_message_buffer);

        // FIFO Client Exist Condition
        if(strcmp(message_buffer, "end") == 0){
           printf("FIFO PIPE is done with sending the data.\n");
           close(file_descriptor);
           exit(1);
        }

        // Prinitng the Data to the Screen that is sent to the Server
        if (end_process != 0) {
           write(file_descriptor, message_buffer, strlen(message_buffer));
           printf("Sent Message: %s\n", message_buffer);
```

```
        } else {
            write(file_descriptor, message_buffer, strlen(message_buffer));
            printf("Sent Message: %s\n", message_buffer);
            close(file_descriptor);
            break;
        }
    }
}
int main() {

    printf("FIFO CLIENT is ready to send the messages to server.\n");
    printf("Enter lines of text, enter \'end\' to quit:\n");

    file_descriptor = open(FIFO_FILE, O_CREAT|O_WRONLY);

    // Function call to send the data to the FIFO.
    sendMessage();

    return 0;
}
```

Figures 6-15 and 6-16 show the output.

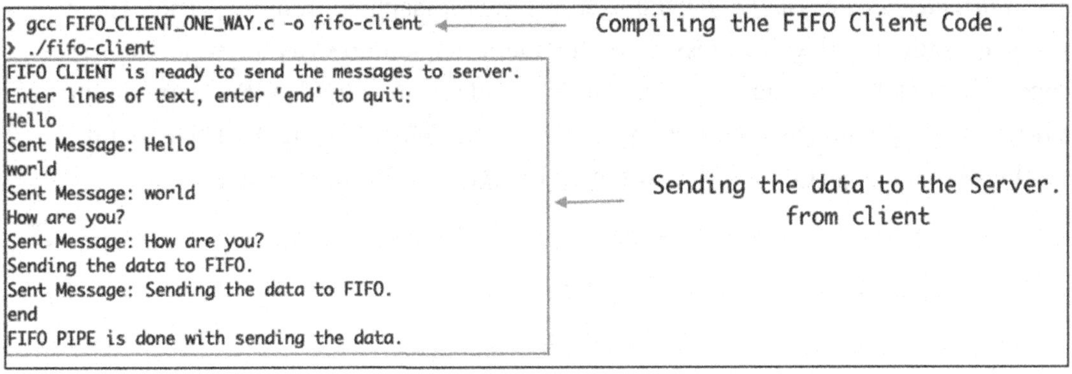

Figure 6-15. *FIFO client program output*

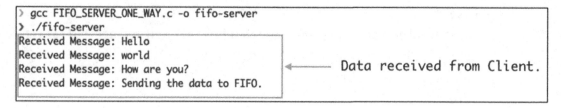

Figure 6-16. *FIFO server program output*

Using Message Queues

Named pipes send data between two processes in a byte-oriented format, which means all the data sent by the process is read character by character. This mechanism is also called a *byte-oriented data transfer mechanism*, which is achieved using the byte stream protocol. The byte-oriented mechanism is a slow process and follows a synchronous data transferring mechanism to achieve the IPC.

The problem with named pipes is that the message/data that is written to the pipe is deleted once the client performs the read operation. So more than one process can't access the data using pipes. Message queues were introduced to avoid this issue. In message queues, the data is stored within the kernel, so you can access the data and process it based on your needs. The data is available for any number of processes until it is deleted explicitly.

A *message queue* is a linked list that stores the messages within the kernel. The message is identified with a message queue identifier. It follows a bidirectional mechanism of data transfer, which is not provided by the named and unnamed pipes. The message queue remains in the system until it is deleted explicitly. The general workflow of message queues is represented in Figure 6-17.

General WorkFlow of Message Queues

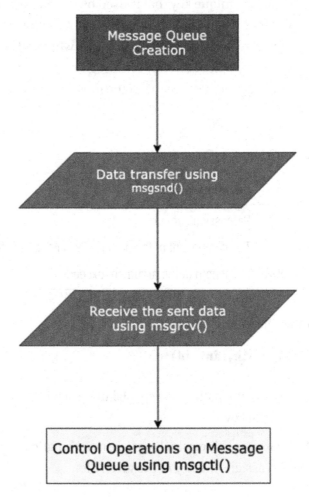

Figure 6-17. *Workflow of message queues*

APIs for Message Queues

Message queues are implemented with the <sys/ipc.h> and <sys/msg.h> libraries. The system calls that quietly perform the IPC using message queues are msgget(), msgsnd(), msgrcv(), and msgctl(). Each system call has a specific purpose in the life cycle of an IPC using message queues.

ftok()

The ftok() system call creates a unique key that is used by the message queues, semaphore, and shared memory. The ftok() system call is available in the <sys/ipc.h> library. The return type of this system call is key_t type, which returns a key that is a positive value. Successful creation of this key returns a unique key value; otherwise, it returns –1 with an error code message. Some of the most common error codes are described in Table 6-3.

Table 6-3. *Common Error Codes*

Error Code	Description
EACCES	Permissions are denied.
ENOTDIR	The component of the path prefix is not a directory.
ENAMETOOLONG	The length of the argument exceeds the size.

The following shows the syntax.

`key_t ftok(const char *path, int id)`

- `path` takes the absolute path of the special file as a parameter to the point with a special key.

- `id` takes the character value, which typecasts automatically into an integer type and assigns the key to the given file.

msgget()

The msgget() system call creates a new message queue identifier or connects with the existing message queue identifier. The return type of this system call is an integer. A successful creation or connection of the message queue identifier returns the value of the message queue identifier, which is a positive value; otherwise, it returns –1 with any one of the error messages in Table 6-4.

Table 6-4. *Error Messages*

Error Code	Description
ENOMEM	No sufficient memory for message queue creation
EEXIST	Message queue already exists
ENOSPC	System limit exceeded for message queue creation
EACCES	Permissions issues with key and message queue identifier

The following shows the syntax.

int msgget(key_t key, int msgflg)

- key takes the unique key that is created using the ftok() system call.

- The msgflag message flag sets the permissions and creates the IPC. If the message queue is ready, it gives an error message with EEXIST code.

msgsnd()

The msgsnd() system call sends data to the message queue using the message buffer object to achieve the IPC. The msgsnd() system call has permissions to write the data to the buffer. The process that calls the msgsnd() system call also needs to have write permissions. The return type of this system call is an integer. It returns 0 if writing data to the buffer was successful; otherwise, it returns –1 with an error code (see Table 6-5).

Table 6-5. *Error Codes*

Error Code	Description
EACCES	If the calling process doesn't have write permissions
EIDRM	Message queue is removed in the middle of the process
ENOMEM	System doesn't have enough memory
EINVAL	Invalid Message Queue Identifier

The following shows the syntax.

```
int msgsnd(int msqid,
           const void *msgp,
           size_t msgsz,
           int msgflg)
```

- msqid takes the message queue identifier, which is created using the msgget() system call.

- The msgp message pointer is the buffer pointer value that takes the message buffer/data that writes to the message queue.

- msqsz takes the size of the message that writes to the message queue. The size is usually represented in bytes.

- The msgflag message flag value is usually set to 0 or ignored; else, you can use IPC_NOWAIT. If the message queue is full, the message buffer does not write any data to the message queue and control returns to the same calling process; otherwise, the calling process suspends or blocks until the message buffer is written to the message queue. If the IPC_NOWAIT flag is not 0, the message does not send, and the calling process returns immediately. If the IPC_NOWAIT flag is 0, then the calling process is suspended until the message queue is removed from the system. For a 0 flag value, you can set custom conditions to make the calling process suspended.

Here is the message buffer structure.

```
struct messageBuffer {
    long messageType;
    char messageText[1];  // Message Data.
};
```

Message Type

messageType is the message type that sends data from the message buffer. This message type communicates with other message types.

- If the message type value is 0, the first message in the queue is read.

- If the message type value is greater than 0, it reads the first message in the queue of type msgtype. For example, if the message type value is 7, it reads only this value, even though other types of messages are available in the message queue.

- If the message type value is less than 0, the first message in the queue with the lowest type less than or equal to the absolute value of the message type is read. For example, if the message type is –7, it reads the first message type that is less than 7 (i.e., a message type from 1 to 7).

Message Text

A message text is a character array that stores the data sent to the message queue.

msgrcv()

The msgrcv() system call receives the data that is written to the message queue. A msgrcv() system call must have read permissions to read the data from the message queue, and the calling process needs to have read permissions. The return type of this system call is ssize_t. If reading data from the message queue is successful, it returns the number of bytes that have read from the queue; otherwise, it throws an error code by returning –1.

The following shows the syntax.

```
ssize_t msgrcv(int msqid,
               void *msgp,
               size_t msgsz,
               long msgtyp,
               int msgflg)
```

- `msqid` takes the message queue identifier, which is created using the msgget() system call.

- The `msgp` message pointer points to the message buffer that is read from the message queue. The received message has a NULL value at the end of the string.

- `msqsz` is the size of the message received from the message queue.

- `msqtyp` indicates the type of message that you want to receive from the queue.

- The `msgflag` message flag value is usually set to 0 or ignored, or you can use IPC_NOWAIT. If this flag is specified when the message queue is full, the message buffer does not write any data to the message queue and control returns to the same calling process; otherwise, the calling process is suspended or blocked until the message buffer is written to the message queue. You can use the MSG_NOERROR flag that truncates the message if the size exceeds.

msgctl()

The msgctl() system call performs the control operations on the message queue. In general, the msgctl() system call destroys the queue. The return type of this system call is an integer. It returns 0 for successful operations and returns –1 if any error/failure occurs. You can use the perror() to get the respective error code.

The following shows the syntax.

`int msgctl(int msqid, int cmd, struct msqid_ds *buf)`

- `msqid` takes the message queue identifier, which is created using the msgget() system call that identifies the message queue.

- The `cmd` flag performs certain operations on message queues using commands or flags. The following are the most common commands used for this parameter.

  - IPC_SET sets the user ID and group ID of the owner and sets the permissions.

  - IPC_INFO returns information about the message queue.

- IPC_RMID immediately removes the message queue from the kernel.

- IPC_STAT provides information about the msqid_ds buffer, which is a part of the same system call.

- MSG_INFO returns information about the msginfo structure and the resources used by the message queue in the system. The structure of the message information is as follows.

```
struct msginfo {

    int msgpool; /* Size in kibibytes of the buffer pool
                    used to hold message data;
                    unused within kernel */

    int msgmap;  /* Maximum number of entries in the
                    Message map; unused within kernel*/

    int msgmax;  /* Maximum number of bytes that can be
                    written in a single message */

    int msgmnb;  /* Maximum number of bytes that can be
                    written to queue; used to initialize
                    msg_qbytes during queue creation
                    (msgget(2)) */

    int msgmni;  /* Maximum number of message queues */

    int msgssz;  /* Message segment size;
                    unused within kernel */

    int msgtql;  /* Maximum number of messages on all
                    Messages in the system; unused within
                    kernel */

    unsigned short int msgseg; /* Maximum number of;
                    segments unused within kernel */

};
```

- The buf argument is a pointer variable that points to the message queue structure named struct msqid_ds. This buffer works based on the commands specified by the user. The msqid_ds data structure is available in <sys/msg.h> as follows.

```
struct msqid_ds {
    struct ipc_perm msg_perm;       // Ownership and permissions
    time_t msg_stime;               // Time of last msgsnd()
    time_t msg_rtime;               // Time of last msgrcv()
    time_t msg_ctime;               /* Creation time/time of last
                                       modification via msgctl() */

    unsigned long __msg_cbytes;     /* Current number of bytes in
                                       queue (nonstandard) */

    msgqnum_t msg_qnum;             /* Current number of messages
                                       in queue */

    msglen_t msg_qbytes;            /* Maximum number of bytes
                                       allowed in queue */

    pid_t msg_lspid;                // PID of last msgsnd()
    pid_t msg_lrpid;                // PID of last msgrcv()
};
```

Let's look at the terms that are used in msqid_ds.

- msg_perm is an ipc_perm structure that describes the permissions of the message queue. The structure of ipc_perm is as follows.

```
struct ipc_perm {
    key_t  __key;           // Key supplied to msgget()
    uid_t  uid;             // Effective UID of owner
    gid_t  gid;             // Effective GID of owner
    uid_t  cuid;            // Effective UID of creator
    gid_t  cgid;            // Effective GID of creator
    unsigned short mode;    // Permissions
    unsigned short __seq;   // Sequence number
};
```

- `msg_qnum` describes the number of messages that are currently available in the message queue. This property is very handy for checking the number of messages in a message queue while writing custom programs.

- `msg_qbytes` describes the maximum number of bytes that are allowed in a message queue for a single message.

- `msg_lspid` provides the ID of the process that calls the msgsnd() system call.

- `msg_lrpid` provides the ID of the process that calls the msgrcv() system call.

- `msg_stime` provides the time taken by the msgsnd() system call to perform the operation.

- `msg_rtime` provides the time taken by the msgrcv() system call to perform the operation.

- `msg_ctime` provides the creation time of the message queue or execution time of the msgctl() system call operation.

Message Queue Implementation

This section looks at the implementation of IPC using message queues by developing sender and receiver applications. This is straightforward once you understand the concepts.

The following is a sender program.

```c
#include <stdio.h>
#include <stdlib.h>
#include <string.h>
#include <string.h>
#include <errno.h>
#include <sys/types.h>
#include <sys/ipc.h>
#include <sys/msg.h>

// Permissions for the Message Queue.
```

```
#define PERMISSIONS 0777

// Definition of Message Buffer
struct messageBuffer {
  long messageType;
  char data[1024];
};

// Global Declaration of Message Buffer Object
struct messageBuffer object;

// Global Data for Variables
int msqid;
int len;
int string_status;
key_t key;

// Function to send the data to the message queue.
void sendMessage(){

  while(fgets(object.data, sizeof object.data, stdin) != NULL) {

      // Calculating the length of the data object.
      len = strlen(object.data);
      if (object.data[len-1] == '\n') object.data[len-1] = '\0';

      // If message queue unable to send the message then
      // below condition Checks and throws an error and exit the message queue.
      if (msgsnd(msqid, &object, len+1, 0) == -1){
         perror("msgsnd");
         exit(1);
      }
      // Checking for the sender exit status.
      string_status = strcmp(object.data, "end");
      if(string_status == 0)
         break;
  }
```

```c
    if (msgctl(msqid, IPC_RMID, NULL) == -1) {
        perror("msgctl");
        exit(1);
    }

    printf("Message Queue is done with sending messages.\n");
}
int main() {

    system("touch messagequeue.txt");

    if ((key = ftok("messagequeue.txt", 'B')) == -1) {
        perror("ftok");
        exit(1);
    }

    if ((msqid = msgget(key, PERMISSIONS | IPC_CREAT)) == -1) {
        perror("msgget");
        exit(1);
    }
    printf("Message Queue is ready to send messages.\n");
    printf("Enter lines of text, enter \'end\' to quit:\n");
    object.messageType = 1; // Setting the message type value to 1.
    // Calling the function to send the data to the message queue.
    sendMessage();

    // Deleting the created file
    system("rm messagequeue.txt");

    return 0;
}
```

The following is a receiver program.

```c
#include <stdio.h>
#include <stdlib.h>
#include<string.h>
#include <errno.h>
#include <sys/types.h>
```

```c
#include <sys/ipc.h>
#include <sys/msg.h>

#define PERMISSIONS 0777

// Definition of Message Buffer
struct messageBuffer {
  long mtype;
  char data[1024];
};

// Global Declaration of Message Buffer Object
struct messageBuffer object;

// Global Data for Variables
int msqid;
int string_status;
key_t key;

// Function to receive the data from message queue.
void receiveMessages(){

  while(1) {
     // Trying to retrieve the data from message queue by checking the condition.
     // If there is any error, while retrieving the data then
     // condition throw an error and exits the function.
     if (msgrcv(msqid, &object, sizeof(object.data), 0, 0) == -1) {
        perror("msgrcv");
        exit(1);
     }

     printf("received: \"%s\"\n", object.data);
     string_status = strcmp(object.data,"end");
     if (string_status == 0)
        break;
  }
}
int main() {
```

```
// Creating the unique Identifier for the message queue.
if ((key = ftok("messagequeue.txt", 'B')) == -1) {
    perror("ftok");
    exit(1);
}
// Connecting the Message Queue.
if ((msqid = msgget(key, PERMISSIONS)) == -1) {
    // connect to the queue
    printf("Unable to Create the Message Queue.\n");
    perror("msgget");
    exit(1);
}

printf("Message Queue is ready to receive messages.\n");
// Calling the receive message function to retrieve the data from the
    message queue.
receiveMessages();

printf("Message Queue is done with receiving messages.\n");
return 0;
}
```

Figures 6-18 and 6-19 show the output.

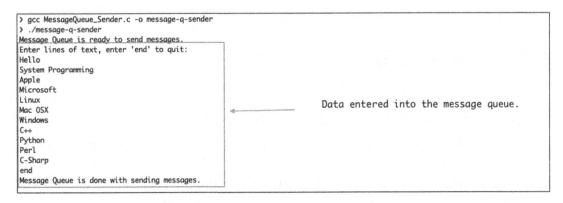

Figure 6-18. *Message queue sender output*

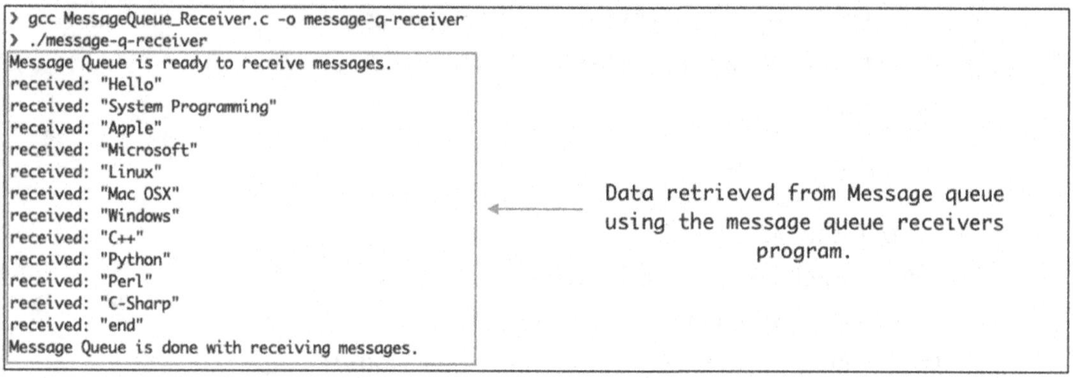

```
> gcc MessageQueue_Receiver.c -o message-q-receiver
> ./message-q-receiver
Message Queue is ready to receive messages.
received: "Hello"
received: "System Programming"
received: "Apple"
received: "Microsoft"
received: "Linux"
received: "Mac OSX"
received: "Windows"
received: "C++"
received: "Python"
received: "Perl"
received: "C-Sharp"
received: "end"
Message Queue is done with receiving messages.
```

Data retrieved from Message queue using the message queue receivers program.

Figure 6-19. *Message queue receiver output*

Introduction to Semaphores

A *semaphore* achieves process synchronization. When two or more processes are using the same resources to perform a task, it may result in improper output. To avoid that problem, a lock keeps the critical section. (A *lock* uses synchronization mechanisms to prevent multiple threads from accessing the same data at the same time. A *critical section* means the common resources shared by multiple processes.)

Dijkstra introduced semaphores to avoid a critical section problem and to achieve process synchronization. A semaphore is a positive integer variable that is shared between threads and processes. A semaphore allows or blocks the resources of a process or thread based on conditions. Semaphores are classified into two types: binary and counting.

Binary Semaphores

Binary means two (i.e., either 0 or 1). A *binary semaphore* has two possible values (i.e., either 0 or 1) that solve the critical section problem for multiple processes. In a binary semaphore, there are two kinds of operations available (i.e., wait and signal operations). If the semaphore value is 1, a wait operation takes place. If the semaphore value is 0, a signaling operation takes place. In a wait operation, the process waits for the resources to be used. In a signal operation, the process is utilizing the available resources.

Counting Semaphores

Counting semaphores control the resources that have multiple instances. A counting semaphore has a value over a certain domain range, and it solves the critical section problem. If the counter value is 0, the resources are unavailable. If the resources are utilizing the process with multiple instances, the counter value is incremented based on the number of instances. If resources are unavailable for the new instance, the value is set to 0.

Characteristics of Semaphores

Here are the characteristics of a semaphore.

- It is a low-level synchronization mechanism for processes.

- A semaphore has a nonnegative integer value.

- It can work with many processes at the same time.

- It synchronizes the global memory that is accessed by many processes/threads.

- Each critical section has a specific semaphore, but that is not mandatory. You can set the same semaphore for multiple critical sections as well.

The Advantages of Using a Semaphore

Here are the advantages of using a semaphore.

- It allows only one thread/process at a time to use the critical section because it uses mutual exclusion.

- It is a machine-independent mechanism.

- It manages resources flexibly.

- It reduces process time and resources because the process, which is in a waiting state, doesn't use processor time to check for the condition to enter the critical section. Semaphores handle everything related to the critical section.

The Disadvantages of Using a Semaphore

Here are the disadvantages of using a semaphore.

- The operating system needs to keep track of all changes done by wait() and signal() calls.

- It may lead to deadlock in certain situations. A deadlock is a situation that usually occurs in an operating system; that is, when a process or thread enters a waiting state because of the unavailability of system resources that are being used by other processes or threads in the system, this situation leads to a deadlock condition. But you can resolve or overcome a deadlock situation with deadlock detection and avoidance algorithms, which are usually called *banker's algorithms*. (The explanation of a banker's algorithm is beyond the scope of this book.)

- Semaphore programming is hard to do.

Semaphore vs. Mutex

Table 6-6 compares a semaphore to a mutex.

Table 6-6. *Comparing a Semaphore to Mutex*

Semaphore	Mutex
It is a signaling mechanism.	It is a locking mechanism.
It is an integer type.	It is an object type.
The modification of a semaphore is done with the wait and signal operations.	The modification is done with the process only.
Resource management is done with the wait and signal operations.	Resource management is done with a locking mechanism.
The semaphore value is changed using wait() and signal() calls.	The mutex value is changed using the lock and unlock mechanisms.
There are two types of semaphores: binary and counting.	A mutex has no subtypes.
You can have multiple program threads at the same time.	You can have multiple program threads at the same time but not simultaneously.

APIs for a Semaphore

Semaphore programming is done with the <sys/sem.h> library. The system calls that are widely used to work with semaphore programming are semget(), semop(), semctl(). This section addresses system calls.

semget()

The semget() system call creates a new semaphore or gets an existing semaphore. The return type of this system call is an integer. It returns the valid semaphore identifier if successful and returns –1 if any failure occurs. When you want to get the respective error code, you need to use the perror() system call.

The following shows the syntax.

```
int semget(key_t key, int nsems, int semflg)
```

- **key** is the first parameter that takes the key value as an argument that identifies the message queue identifier. The key is either set manually or created by ftok() system call.

- **nsems** takes the parameter of the number of semaphores. In a binary semaphore, 1 implies the need for one semaphore set. In a counting semaphore based on the count, the number of semaphores is added.

- The **semflg** parameter deals with the flags required to create the semaphore and the permissions that are set for the newly created semaphore.

semop()

The semop() system call acquires or releases the semaphore. This system call deals with resource allocation and freeing the resources. The return type of this system call is an integer. It returns 0 if successful and returns –1 if any failure occurs.

The following shows the syntax.

```
int semop(int semid,
          struct sembuf *semops,
          size_t nsemops)
```

209

- **semid** takes the semaphore identifier that is created using the semget() system call.

- **semops** is a pointer to an array of operations that must be performed on the semaphore. The structure variable is as follows.

```
struct sembuf {
  unsigned short sem_num; // Semaphore set num
  short sem_op;           // Semaphore operation
  short sem_flg;          // Operation flags, IPC_NOWAIT, SEM_UNDO
};
```

In this structure, sem_op represents the semaphore operation that needs to be performed.

- If the sem_op value is negative, then semaphore obtains or allocates the resources to the processes.

- If the sem_op value is positive, then the semaphore releases the resources.

- If the sem_op value is 0, then the calling process waits until the semaphore value reaches 0.

- **nsemops** represents the number of operations to perform on that array.

semctl()

The semctl() system call performs various operations on the semaphore. The operations include getting and setting information about the semaphore. semctl() also removes the semaphore from the operating system. The return type of this system call is an integer. It returns a positive integer if successful and returns –1 if any error occurs.

The following shows the syntax.

`int semctl(int semid, int semnum, int cmd, ...)`

- **semid** is a semaphore identifier value that is created using a semget() system call, which uniquely identifies the semaphore on an operating system.

- **semnum** deals with the number of semaphores counted; the value starts at 0.

- **cmd** takes the command that you want to perform on a semaphore.

Accessing Global Data Without Semaphores

This section presents a simple example that accesses global data without a semaphore using multiple threads, and shows how this leads to inconsistency in data.

```c
#include<stdio.h>
#include<stdlib.h>
#include<unistd.h>
#include<pthread.h>

// Global Data variables.
int a = 5, b = 7;

// Function that access the global data.
void* add_two_numbers(void* arg){
    a = a + 3;
    b = b - 1;
    printf("a value is: %d and ", a);
    printf("b value is: %d\n", b);
    sleep(1);
    exit(0);
}

int main(){

    // Creating the thread instances.
    pthread_t t1, t2, t3;

    pthread_create(&t1, NULL, add_two_numbers, NULL);
    pthread_create(&t2, NULL, add_two_numbers, NULL);
    pthread_create(&t3, NULL, add_two_numbers, NULL);

    pthread_join(t1, NULL);
    pthread_join(t2, NULL);
    pthread_join(t3, NULL);
```

```
//Destroying the threads.
pthread_exit(t1);
pthread_exit(t2);
pthread_exit(t3);
return 0;
}
```

In this code example, the add_two_numbers function acts like a critical section. Three threads are trying to access the global data of a and b. Since there is no proper locking mechanism for global data, this leads to race conditions and inconsistent results. The result of the program is shown in Figure 6-20.

```
> gcc RaceCondition.c
> ./a.out                                  The values of a and b
a value is: 8 and b value is: 4    doesn't give accurate results as expected
a value is: 14 and b value is: 4  ←   after performing the Operations by
a value is: 11 and b value is: 4           three different threads.
```

Figure 6-20. *Race condition program output*

Implementing the Data Consistent Model Using a Semaphore and a Mutex

This section implements a semaphore and a mutex to achieve process and thread synchronization.

```
#include<stdio.h>
#include<stdlib.h>
#include<unistd.h>
#include<pthread.h>
#include<semaphore.h>

sem_t mutex;

int a = 5, b = 7;
// Function to access the global data
void* add_two_numbers(void* arg){
    sem_wait(&mutex);
```

```
    a = a + 3;
    b = b - 1;
    printf("a value is: %d and ", a);
    printf("b value is: %d\n", b);
    sleep(1);
    sem_post(&mutex);
}

int main(){
    sem_init(&mutex, 0, 1);
    pthread_t t1, t2, t3;
    pthread_create(&t1, NULL, add_two_numbers, NULL);
    sleep(1);
    pthread_create(&t2, NULL, add_two_numbers, NULL);
    sleep(1);
    pthread_create(&t3, NULL, add_two_numbers, NULL);
    sleep(1);

    pthread_join(t1, NULL);
    pthread_join(t2, NULL);
    pthread_join(t3, NULL);
    sem_destroy(&mutex);

    return 0;
}
```

In this example, you used a semaphore to synchronize global data. The problem that occurred due to a race condition is solved with a semaphore. Since you are using a semaphore, there is no loss in data, as shown in Figure 6-21.

```
> ./semaphore
a value is: 8 and b value is: 6                There is no data loss
a value is: 11 and b value is: 5   ◄────   and also we got the results
a value is: 14 and b value is: 4                   as expected.
```

Figure 6-21. *Semaphore and mutex program output*

Summary

This chapter discussed various IPC techniques and how to achieve them using C programming. The code samples and topics covered in this chapter should help you better understand interprocess communication.

- Anonymous pipes share data in a unidirectional way.

- Named pipes build a client-server-based application.

- Message queues build a client-server architecture within an operating system.

- Semaphores better synchronize processes, especially in critical sections.

The upcoming chapters discuss other IPC techniques, including shared memory and sockets.

CHAPTER 7

Shared Memory

Shared memory is a highly efficient way of sharing data between running processes or programs. It allows two or more unrelated processes to access the logical memory segment. Sharing a common piece of the memory segment is the fastest way that IPC can be achieved. This chapter covers the following topics, which include code samples.

- Introduction to shared memory

- The API for shared memory

- Kernel support for shared memory

- Implementation of shared memory

Introduction to Shared Memory

Shared memory occurs among multiple processes. Communication between processes is done in a commonly shared memory region. All other processes can view any change made by a single process. It is one of the fastest forms of IPC available because, in a shared memory mechanism, data is not copied from one address space to another address space. Also, memory allocation happens only once in shared memory, which is the reason it's is faster than other forms of IPC techniques. Processes accessing shared memory have a separate address space. All the processes are independent of each other, but they are dependent on the commonly shared memory region. The architecture of shared memory is represented in Figure 7-1.

S. M. Palakollu, *Practical System Programming with C*, https://doi.org/10.1007/978-1-4842-6321-1_7

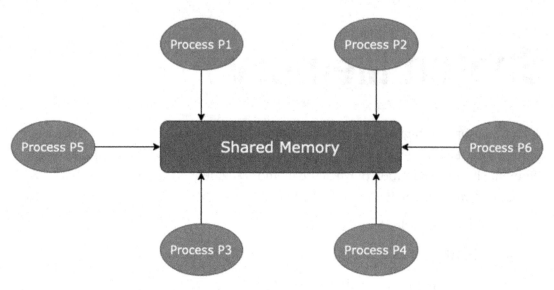

Figure 7-1. *Architecture of shared memory*

The problem with other IPC mechanisms is that when two or more processes want to exchange data, that data needs to be copied to the kernel. The data architecture of other IPC mechanism is explained in Figure 7-2. The process that occurs in other IPC techniques is explained as follows.

1. Initially, the server reads the data/input file. The kernel reads the data into memory and then copies it into the process.

2. After data is loaded into the buffer, the server writes it in a message using the IPC technique (i.e., pipes, FIFO, message queues).

3. The client reads the message with the IPC channel. It requires data to be copied from the kernel IPC buffer to the client buffer.

4. Finally, the data is copied from the client buffer.

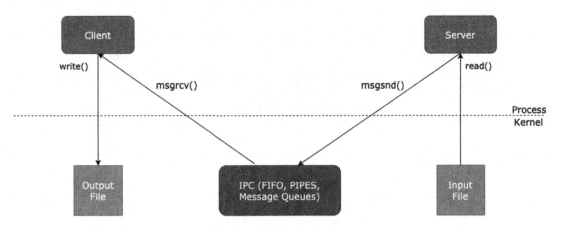

Figure 7-2. *The flow of Data in other IPC Techniques*

Shared memory offers a better way by providing access to two or more processes—a common memory region. Synchronization is required for the shared memory segment when there is no synchronization of the data that is being accessed by multiple processes. This leads to inconsistency in data access, which leads to a race condition. The flow of data in a shared memory segment is represented in Figure 7-3.

- The server accesses the shared memory segment as a semaphore object.

- The server reads the data from the user/input file into the shared memory segment by performing the read operation.

- When the read operation is done, the server notifies the client using the semaphore object.

- The client writes the data from the memory segment to the output file.

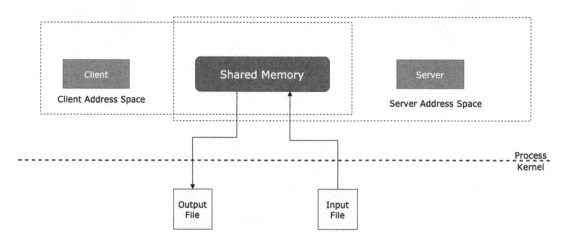

Figure 7-3. *The flow of data in shared memory*

API for Shared Memory

Shared memory is implemented with the <sys/shm.h> library. The system calls that quietly perform the IPC through shared memory are shmget(), shmat(), shmdt(), and shmctl(). Each system call has a specific purpose in the IPC process life cycle.

shmget()

The shmget() system call creates the shared memory segment in an operating system. It also obtains the previously created shared memory segment in the operating system. The return type is an integer type. This system call returns a valid shared memory identifier on success and returns –1 on failure. If you want to get the respective error code, you need to use the perror() system call.

The following shows the syntax.

int shmget(key_t key, size_t size, int shmflg)

- The **key** parameter identifies the shared memory segment in the operating system. The value of the key is arbitrary, or it is created using the ftok() system call.

- The **size** parameter takes the size of the shared memory segment.

- The **shmflg** parameter takes the parameters to create the shared memory segment and the permissions set for the shared memory on the system.

shmat()

The shmat() system call attaches the shared memory segment to the address space of the calling process. When you want to use the created shared memory, you need to attach the shared memory segment with the calling process address space. The return type is a void pointer return type. It returns the address of the shared memory segment attached segment and returns –1 if any failure occurs.

The following shows the syntax.

```
void * shmat(int shmid,
             const void *shmaddr,
             int shmflg)
```

- shmid takes the shared memory identifier as an argument created using the shmget() system call. This identifier value helps the shmat() system call properly attach the calling process.

- shmaddr takes the attaching address as an argument. If you set the address as NULL, then by default, the system assigns the suitable address for attaching the segment. If the address value is not NULL, then you can set the address value based on shmflg.

- shmflg takes certain parameters to manipulate the shared memory segment and the address space value.

Table 7-1. *Flags*

Flag Value	Description
SHM_RDONLY	This flag attaches the shared memory segment for the read-only purpose only.
SHM_RND	It rounds off the address space to the SHMLBA (shared memory lower boundary address).
SHM_EXEC	It allows the shared memory segment to be executed.

shmdt()

The shmdt() system call detaches the shared memory segment from the address space of the calling process. The return type is an integer type. It returns 0 on the successful detachment of the address space and returns –1 if any failure occurs.

The following shows the syntax.

int shmdt(const void *shmaddr)

shmaddr takes the address of the shared memory that needs to be detached from the address space. The value must be the address that is returned by the shmat() system call.

shmctl()

The shmctl() system call performs the various operations on the shared memory segment. It is also used to destroy the shared memory segment after the work is done. The return of this system call is an integer type. It returns 0 on successful operations and returns –1 if any error occurs.

The following shows the syntax.

int shmctl(int shmid, int cmd, struct shmid_ds *buf)

- shmid takes the identifier of the shared memory segment that is created using the shmget() system call. The operations and the destroying of shared memory activity be performed on the given shared memory identifier.

- cmd takes the command to perform the operations on the shared memory segment. The commands that can be passed to this argument are shown in Table 7-2.

- **buf** is a pointer to the shmid_ds data structure. It works as per the cmd argument.

Table 7-2. *Commands*

Command	Description
IPC_STAT	It copies the information from the kernel data structure.
IPC_SET	It sets the user ID and group ID for the owner. It also deals with permissions.
IPC_RMID	It destroys the segment.
IPC_INFO	It gets information about the shared memory segment.
SHM_INFO	It gets information about system resource usage.

Kernel Support for Shared Memory

POSIX-based systems support shared memory to achieve IPC. The kernel supports shared memory with a predefined data structure. There is a shared memory table available in the kernel address space. It keeps track of all the shared memory segments in the system. Each entry of the table stores the following data.

- Name of the shared memory segment

- User ID and group ID of the creator

- Assigned owner and group ID

- Permissions of the shared memory segment

- Information about the process attached to the region

- Information about the process detached from the region

- Information about the operations done to the region

- Size of the memory segment

The kernel structure for the shared memory data structure is as follows.

```
struct shmid_ds {
    struct ipc_perm shm_perm;    // Ownership and permissions
    size_t shm_segsz;            // Size of segment (bytes)
    time_t shm_atime;            // Last attach time
    time_t shm_dtime;            // Last detach time
```

```
    time_t shm_ctime;          /* Creation time/time of last
                                  modification via shmctl() */
    pid_t shm_cpid;            // PID of creator
    pid_t shm_lpid;            // PID of last shmat()/shmdt()
    shmatt_t shm_nattch;       // No. of current attaches
};
```

The structure of ipc_perm is as follows.

```
struct ipc_perm {
    key_t  __key;              // Key supplied to shmget()
    uid_t  uid;                // Effective UID of owner
    gid_t  gid;                // Effective GID of owner
    uid_t  cuid;               // Effective UID of creator
    gid_t  cgid;               // Effective GID of creator
    unsigned short mode;       /* Permissions + SHM_DEST and
                                  SHM_LOCKED flags */
    unsigned short __seq; // Sequence number
};
```

Implementation of Shared Memory

This section implements shared memory by using two separate programs. One program writes the data into the memory, and the other program reads the data from memory.

Shared Memory Writers Program

In the shared memory writer program, a shared memory segment is created with a shmget() system call. Data is written to the memory segment by attaching it with the shmat() system call. The writer's program writes the data into the memory segment, which is accessed by using the reader program.

```
#include<stdio.h>
#include<string.h>
#include <sys/ipc.h>
#include <sys/shm.h>
```

```c
int main() {
  // ftok to generate unique key
  key_t key = ftok("memory",67);
   // shmget returns an identifier in shmid
  int shmid = shmget(key, 1024,0666|IPC_CREAT);

  if(shmid == -1){
      printf("Unable to create the Shared Memory Segment.\n");
  }

  // shmat to attach to shared memory
  char *str = (char*) shmat(shmid,(void*)0,0);
   printf("Enter Data to write into the Shared Memory Segment: ");
  scanf("%[^\n]s", str);
   printf("Data written in memory: %s\n",str);

  //detach from shared memory
  shmdt(str);
   return 0;
}
```

Shared Memory Reader Program

In a shared memory reader program, the data that is written to the memory segment
is read with the shmat() system call. Once the use of the shared memory segment is
done, you can detach the memory segment and destroy it. Once the memory segment is
detached and destroyed, it can't access it again.

```c
#include <stdio.h>
#include <sys/ipc.h>
#include <sys/shm.h>
 int main() {

   // ftok to generate unique key
   key_t key = ftok("memory",67);
    // shmget returns an identifier in shmid
   int shmid = shmget(key, 1024,0666|IPC_CREAT);
```

```
if(shmid == -1){
    printf("Unable to Connect with the shared memory segment.\n");
}
// shmat to attach to shared memory
char *str = (char*) shmat(shmid,(void*)0,0);
 printf("Data read from memory: %s\n",str);

//detach from shared memory
shmdt(str);

// destroy the shared memory
shmctl(shmid,IPC_RMID,NULL);

    return 0;
}
```

Figure 7-4 shows the output.

```
> gcc Shared\ Memory\ Writer.c -o writer  ←————————        Writer Program Execution.
> ./writer
Enter Data to write into the Shared Memory Segment: Practical System Programming with C...!
Data written in memory: Practical System Programming with C...!  ←————    Data written into the Shared Memory Segment.
> gcc Shared\ Memory\ Reader.c -o reader  ←————————     Execution of Reader Program
> ./reader
Data read from memory: Practical System Programming with C...!  ←————    Data read from the Shared Memory Segment.
```

Figure 7-4. *The output of the Shared Memory Writers and Readers program*

Summary

This chapter discussed shared memory, which shares a large amount of data through a common memory region. The problem with shared memory and IPC mechanisms like pipes, message queues, and semaphores is that the sharing of data is done only within the operating system. When you want to share the data outside the system, it is achieved with socket programming. Socket programming is discussed in the next chapter.

CHAPTER 8

Socket Programming

Socket programming is a way of connecting two nodes on a network to communicate with each other. It achieves the IPC over a network. The following topics and code samples are covered in this chapter.

- Introduction to sockets

- IPC over network

- Generic API for socket programming

- OSI architectural model

- TCP/IP model

- Client-server architecture

- Implementation of client-server architecture using TCP protocol

- Implementation of client-server architecture using UDP protocol

Introduction to Sockets

A socket is a bidirectional gateway that communicates with different processes on the same machine or different machines. In Unix/Linux, it is a file descriptor that establishes a network connection with real-world applications. Real-world applications like telnet, FTP, and other popular network services use sockets for establishing a connection and for sending and receiving data.

A socket is a combination of an IP address and a port number. A port number/port is a communication endpoint that connects with an external device. When you send a request to a website using the HTTP protocol, by default, you are trying to connect and establish a connection with that website through port 80.

© Sri Manikanta Palakollu 2021
S. M. Palakollu, *Practical System Programming with C*, https://doi.org/10.1007/978-1-4842-6321-1_8

Sockets build client-server architecture systems. The client-server architecture is discussed later in this chapter.

Sockets transfer data between systems using a remote IP address and the port number. Some application-level protocols like POP3, FTP, and popular mail services use sockets to establish a connection with remote systems/servers. The types of sockets available are differentiated based on data transfer mechanisms.

Stream Sockets

Packet delivery flow follows the order of *stream sockets*. When a socket transfers data, it converts the data into packets to transfer to the remote system. In this stream socket mechanism, all the data packets deliver effectively without any loss. It uses a connection-oriented approach for data transfer. The underlying protocol used by this socket methodology is TCP (Transmission Control Protocol). Stream sockets guarantee data delivery in any case. If the packets are impossible to deliver, it generates an error message to the receiver with a negative acknowledgment.

Datagram Sockets

The data delivery mechanism in a *datagram socket* is completely different from the stream socket mechanism. In a datagram socket mechanism, the data delivery does not follow the order the packets may arrive in any order to the receiver. The underlying protocol used by the datagram socket system is UDP (User Datagram Protocol). This system doesn't guarantee that data gets to the receiver. It is a connectionless approach for data transfer.

Raw Sockets

Raw sockets use a datagram sockets mechanism. But the characteristics of this protocol are completely dependent on the interface provided by the protocol. Raw sockets are intended for advanced users who want to take advantage of the protocol features that are not directly accessible from the general interface. These sockets also develop new protocols on top of the existing protocols.

Domain Sockets

Domain sockets provide a medium to communicate with the processes of the same host system. Stream and datagram sockets are the generic sockets that provide an abstract layer for communication. But you need domain sockets to use them in various domains. In this chapter, you are working with the Unix sockets because it supports the POSIX standards. To implement IPC in Unix-based systems, domain-level sockets are required.

Internet Domain Sockets

Unix sockets are communicate only with other process in the same system. When you want to communicate with remote systems, advanced protocols that can establish a connection with remote systems are required. Internet domain sockets communicate with the other processes available in remote systems. The underlying protocol used by Internet domain sockets is the TCP/IP protocol (Transmission Control Protocol/Internet Protocol). An Internet protocol is a low-level protocol that sends data through the Internet by splitting and joining data packets. A TCP protocol works on top of the IP protocol to guarantee that the data packets get to the receiver.

IPC Over Network

Interprocess communication happens over a network with sockets. When you are designing your socket server to establish an IPC activity, it should follow certain guidelines.

- Communication style
- Namespaces
- Protocols

Communication Style

Communication style deals with how data should transfer over the network. When data is transferring through the socket, it is divided into small packets during transmission. On the receiver side, the small packets are grouped to make the complete data. This is called a *transferring mechanism*. It is only applicable to connection-oriented protocols like TCP, whereas it doesn't apply to connectionless protocols like UDP.

Namespaces

Namespaces deal with the type of connection system that transfers the data (i.e., stream socket, datagram socket, etc.). It determines the connection style of the data transfer. If you use a stream socket connection, it guarantees data delivery to the receiver through a connection-oriented approach.

A *connection-oriented approach* is a methodology that connects the communication devices before transferring data, and after that, it transfers data between systems. The data is delivered to the receiver in the same order that it was sent. It determines the approach of the data transfer and connection establishment between the systems.

Protocol

Two or more entities in a network wanting to communicate requires a standard protocol. A *protocol* is a set of rules and procedures to follow when two entities want to communicate with each other in a network. A protocol consists of error recovery mechanisms and synchronization mechanisms. When IPC needs to occur over a network, protocols are mandatory. The protocols that are typically used are TCP and UDP.

API for Socket Programming

To implement socket programming or achieve IPC over a network, you need to consider the various guidelines that you must follow. But when you want to implement those features and make use of their benefits, you need an appropriate API/library that reduces your development time. In C programming, the <sys/socket.h> library implements socket programming. Generic sockets are also called *Berkeley sockets*, which provide access to interprocess communication services. The workflow of applications that want to communicate over a network using sockets is diagrammatically represented in Figure 8-1.

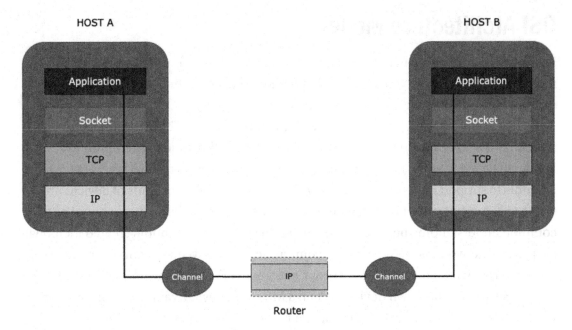

Figure 8-1. *Application connection architecture*

Let's consider two hosts that want to communicate with each other over a network using sockets. The communication is established as follows.

- Host A (sender) creates a socket object with a destination/foreign address and destination/foreign ports that create a socket descriptor. This socket provides an interface to establish communication.

- A socket descriptor is a simple interface, but when you want to establish communication with a remote machine, a protocol is required. The protocol might be UDP/TCP. TCP is a connection-oriented protocol, where UDP is a connectionless protocol.

- When all the protocol rules are assigned to the socket properly, it uses IP to transfer the data/message to a remote machine. The data transfer is done with a router/LAN.

This architectural model is the core model to establish a connection with the remote systems using sockets.

OSI Architecture Model

When two computers want to communicate with each other a network medium is requried. In modern life, you usually use the Internet to communicate with other systems around the world.

When a computer wants to connect with the Internet to establish a connection, it requires a *network adaptor* or *network interface controller*, which are commonly known as *network cards*. The operating system provides drivers to work with network adaptors to support network communication. When two different kinds of devices are trying to communicate with each other through a network medium, there should be a common understanding between both parties. In earlier days, vendors created their own proprietary network models to provide communication between systems over a network.

Suppose that Microsoft creates a proprietary network model for communication over a network for their own devices. When a Microsoft device wants to communicate with another company's device, it causes an issue because other companies use other network proprietary models for their communication purposes. This causes a incompatible communication issue. Another problem with this approach is that when a new network model is introduced at the same company, the older model is not compatible with the new model, which causes a huge communication gap.

To provide a good standard for communication between a wide range of software and hardware devices, OSI layered architecture was introduced. OSI stands for Open System Interconnect, which was developed by ISO in 1984. It is a seven-layered architecture, as shown in the diagram in Figure 8-2. Each layer has a specific functionality and task associated with it. This architecture makes communication better because every system is using a common set of guidelines for communication. There is no need to bother about the hardware, software, or system the other person is using.

There are several different types of protocols available to perform communication over the network but OSI is the standard system model. Protocols like FTP and HTTP can be embedded into this model.

Seven Layers Of OSI

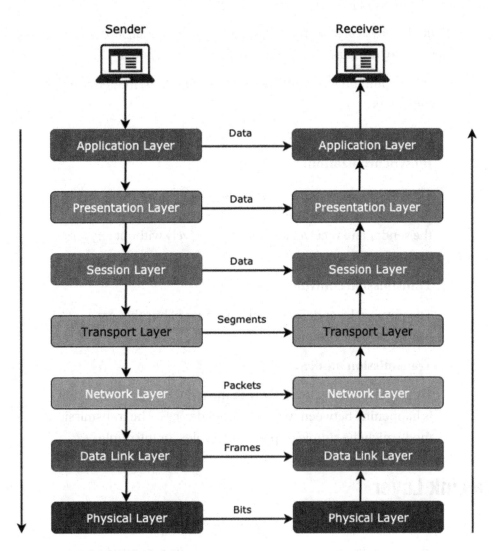

Figure 8-2. *OSI layered architecture*

Physical Layer

The physical layer is the lowest layer of the OSI layered architecture.

- It is also called the *hardware layer*.

- It is responsible for making the physical connection between two parties over a network.

- This layer transfers the information in the form of electrical signal bits (i.e., 0 and 1).

- When the physical layer receives data from the sender, it transfers that data to the data link layer in the form of binary data.

- The most common physical layer devices are cables, modems, hubs, and repeaters.

- The following are the physical layer's functions.

  - **Bit synchronization:**

    The physical layer provides good synchronization for the data bits using clock synchronization. This synchronization helps the sender and receiver send data effectively without any loss in data between transmission.

  - **Transmission control:**

    The physical layer deals with the number of bits that are transmitting per second.

  - **Transmission mode:**

    The physical layer also deals with the type of transmission that is happening between two connected devices. The transmission mode might be simple duplex, half duplex, or full duplex.

Data Link Layer

This data link layer is responsible from node to node to delivery.

- The data is converted into frames in the *data link layer* to make an error-free transmission. A *frame* is a data unit that consists of the MAC address of the sender and receiver associated with the data.

- Devices in the data link layer are switches and bridges.

- The data link layer is divided into two sublayers.

  - Media access layer

  - Logic link layer

- The main functionality of the data link layer is to provide error-free data from one node to another node.

- The following are data link layer functionalities.

  - **Error control:**

    It provides the error control mechanism by using standard algorithms to transmit error-free data.

  - **Flow control:**

    The data link layer provides a flow control mechanism to transmit data between two nodes at a constant speed rate.

  - **Framing:**

    One of the core functionalities of the data link layer is framing. It provides a better way to transmit data between both parties. All data bits are converted into frames by adding extra bits at the beginning and end of the frame. This frame is transmitted at once to another node at a constant speed.

  - **Physical addressing:**

    The data present in this layer is converted into frames. While converting the data into frames, the layer adds a physical MAC address to the data's header section at both the sender and receiver sides. Each data frame has a physical address.

Network Layer

This layer transmits data between multiple hosts that are located on the same or different networks.

- Routers are the hardware devices used in this layer.

- Data is converted into packets in this layer.

- All the packets are sent to other host devices through the network using *routing algorithms*. Routing algorithms decide the best route for a data packet to reach the required destination station.

- Routing algorithms help packets reach the destination host by using the shortest path. Sometimes this changes based on the algorithm and network traffic. Routing algorithms and its issues are beyond the scope of this book.

- The network layer adds a logical address at the header section of a packet.

- The following are the main functionalities of the network layer.

  - **Logical addressing:**

    Logical addressing uniquely identifies packets in the network with IP addresses.

  - **Routing:**

    Routing helps packets reach their destination by using the shortest path.

Transport Layer

The main functionality of the *transport layer* is to provide services to the application layer.

- This layer converts data into segments.

- It is the heart of the OSI-layered architecture because of its end-to-end delivery mechanism.

- It provides end-to-end delivery for the entire application.

- On the sender side, the transport layer receives data from the top layers and converts it into segments. It adds the source and destination port number in the header section and transmits to the network layer.

- On the receiver side, the data is collected from the network layer. It converts the data into segments, reads the port address from the header section, and sends it to the respective application.

- It provides the two kinds of services to the user.

- **Connection-oriented services:**

  In this service, data is transmitted based on the acknowledgment. It is a more secure way of transmitting data. There is no loss in data. It is a slow process for transferring data between devices. The connection has three different phases.

  - Connection establishment

  - Data transfer

  - Connection termination

- **Connectionless service:**

  In this service, data is transmitted without acknowledgment. There is a chance of losing data while transferring. Since there are no optimization techniques in connectionless mode, data is transferred much faster between devices. The data transferred through this mode is called a *datagram*. The frequently used protocols in a connectionless service are UDP and IP. These protocols are stateless.

- The following are the functionalities of the transport layer.

  - **Port addressing:**

    The transport layer adds the source and destination port address in the header section to successfully deliver the proper host machine.

Session Layer

The *session layer* is responsible for connection establishment, sessions, and authentication.

- This layer provides security for the data that is transmitted by using standard authentication protocols for connection establishment. If you use a weak authentication protocol in the session layer, it may lead to malicious brute force attacks.

- It is a software layer.

- The session layer provides good session management. These sessions establish and terminate a connection between two devices.

Presentation Layer

The presentational layer is responsible for encryption and decryption of the data that is being transmitted.

- This layer is also called a *translation layer*.

- The following are the functionalities of the presentation layer.

    - **Encryption:**

        The transferred data is encrypted at the sender's side to provide good security for the data. Encryption is the process of converting plain text into ciphertext.

    - **Decryption:**

        The received data needs to be decrypted at the receiver's side to return it to normal data.

Application Layer

The *application layer* acts as an interface for the end user. This layer is responsible for transferring and receiving the data through the network. All the data transferred to or received from the remote system display in this layer only.

- This layer usually has software-based or command-line based applications that interact with remote machines.

- The applications used in this layer for transmitting and receiving data include browsers, Skype, Messenger, mail delivery services, and so forth.

- The end-user applications must use proper application standards while in development to ensure proper security for the user.

Advantages of the OSI Model

- It provides common guidelines for transferring data between two parties.

- Network hardware does not need to be from the same vendor.

- It is considered a generic model for communication over a network.

- It allows you to communicate between various software and hardware parties with generic rules.

- It helps network administrators easily troubleshoot network issues.

- It adopts different types of protocols.

- It provides both connection-oriented and connectionless services.

Disadvantages of the OSI Model

- It is a complex and theoretical model that doesn't have any practical implementation.

- Addressing duplication of services (i.e., error control, flow control, and data) is done at various layers.

- It is very difficult to fit protocols into this model. Since it is a generic model, it is your responsibility to fit the protocol.

- The session and presentation layers have less functionality than other layers.

- The layers cannot work in parallel because each layer needs to wait to obtain data from another layer.

TCP/IP Architecture Model

The OSI model is a theoretical model that does not have any practical implementation. This model is considered a reference model for developing networking applications. The OSI model divided a logical group of functionalities into simple components to make it more effective for network troubleshooting. Network administrators can easily troubleshoot issues in the OSI model. The problem with the OSI model is that it is just a reference model. Everything must be done from scratch, and some functionalities have duplicates in multiple layers.

The US Department of Defense (DOD) designed TCP/IP in 1960. TCP and IP are different protocols. TCP is a connection-oriented transport protocol that ensures the data delivery of a packet. IP is a connectionless protocol that is responsible for transferring data packets to devices in a network.

TCP/IP was invented before the OSI model. TCP/IP uses the Internet for data transmission. This model consists of four layers. Each layer is logically grouped into units. The following are the layers that are included in this model.

- Network access layer

- Internet layer

- Transport layer

- Application layer

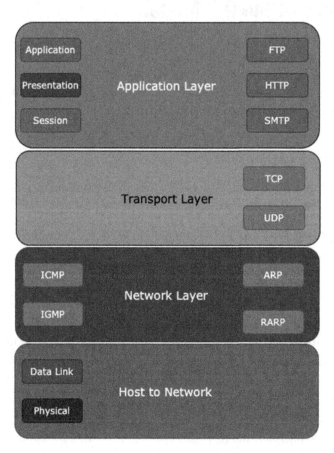

Figure 8-3. *TCP/IP model*

Network Access Layer

The network access layer groups the data link and physical layers.

- It is the lowest layer of the TCP/IP model.

- This layer deals with the physical data transmission between two devices on the same network.

- The main functionalities of the network access layer are the mapping IP addresses into physical addresses. The physical address is the MAC address of your system.

Internet Layer

The Internet layer is the second layer of the TCP/IP protocol. It transfers data over the same network.

- It is also called a *network layer*.

- The protocols that transfer the data over the network are as follows.

  - ICMP: Internet Control Message Protocol

  - ARP: Address Resolution Protocol

  - RARP: Reverse Address Resolution Protocol

  - IGMP: Internet Group Management Protocol

- These are the functionalities of this layer.

  - **Host-to-host communication:**

    It transfers the data to different hosts within a network. The data that is transferred through this layer requires a certain path to transfer. One of the key functionalities of the Internet layer is identifying the path to transfer the data.

  - **Routing:**

    When the data is transferred within the same network, direct data delivery is possible. But when the host is on a different network, direct delivery is not possible. Routing provides an efficient and reliable data transmission for different hosts.

- **Data formatting:**

  In the Internet layer, the data to be transferred needs to be formatted for *lossless data transmission*. Lossless data transmission means the data transferred from the sender to the receiver is not lost during transmission. To make lossless data transmission, data is encapsulated into units. *Encapsulation of data* is the binding of data into a single unit.

Transport Layer

The transport layer is responsible for error-free data delivery to receivers.

- It determines how much data should transfer between the nodes.

- It also determines the number of bits that are transferring per second.

- This layer acknowledges that the data was transferred successfully. Acknowledgment is only available in connection-oriented protocols like TCP. When it comes to connectionless protocols like UDP, there is no acknowledgment.

- These are the protocols that are used in this layer.

  - TCP: Transmission Control Protocol is a connection-oriented protocol. This protocol efficiently sends data without any errors. It is a reliable protocol for data transmission. It has a flow and error control mechanism.

  - UDP: User Datagram Protocol is a connectionless protocol. It does not have the features provided by TCP, but it is more cost-effective and transfers the data very fastly. It is not a reliable protocol.

- The functionalities offered by the transport layer are as follows.

  - **Flow control:** It manages the rate of data transmission between the nodes.

  - **Error control:** It uses the error control mechanism to transfer error-free data for the nodes.

- **Segmentation:** It divides data into several segments before transferring it to the other nodes. It reduces the duplication of data.

- **Desegmentation:** After data is received from the sender, it is desegmented to make it original data. This makes the data transfer in sequence. It is not the same as encryption and decryption.

Application Layer

The application layer interacts with application programs.

- It is the highest level of the TCP/IP model.

- This layer consists of application, session, and presentation layers.

- It is responsible for node-to-node data delivery.

- The protocols that are used in this layer are

  - FTP: File Transfer Protocol

  - SMTP: Simple Mail Transfer Protocol

  - NTP: Network Time Protocol

  - HTTP: Hypertext Transfer Protocol

  - HTTPS: Hypertext Transfer Protocol with SSL Certificate

  - DNS: domain name server

- The applications used in this layer are Skype, email services, remote logins, and so forth.

- The protocols in this layer are the most common, but there are many other types available. If you want, you can implement your own protocol.

Advantages of TCP/IP

The following are the advantages of TCP/IP.

- It is an open source protocol suite model.

- It establishes a connection between two systems.

- It supports different types of routing protocols.

- It does not depend on a device's operating system or hardware.

- It is a scalable architecture for communication.

- It assigns a unique IP address for each device in the network.

- It uses flow control, error control, and congestion control mechanisms for better data transmission. These mechanisms are only applicable for connection-oriented protocols like TCP. They are not applicable for a connectionless protocol like UDP.

- It guarantees the data without any duplication and provides better throughput.

Disadvantages of TCP/IP

The following are the disadvantages of TCP/IP.

- It is not a generic protocol like the OSI model.

- It is complex to set up and use.

- Adopting new protocols and new technologies is very difficult.

Client-Server Architecture

Let's look at client-server architecture.

Client

An application that tries to access the resources from the server by sending the appropriate request to the server from his device is called a *client*. A client may be in any location in the world. It sends a request to access data through a network/the Internet. Devices that run as a client include tablets, mobile devices, laptops, and desktops .

Server

A *server* is a computer program or device that provides services to clients by rendering requests. Some common examples are web servers like Apache, Tomcat, and Jellyfish. Proxy servers, HTTP servers, file servers, and database servers are also examples.

Examining the Client-Server Architecture

In client-server architecture, a client sends a request to the server through a network. Then, the server handles the client's request and answers with a suitable response.

When the client sends a bad request to the server (i.e., the data is unavailable on the server), the server replies with an error message.

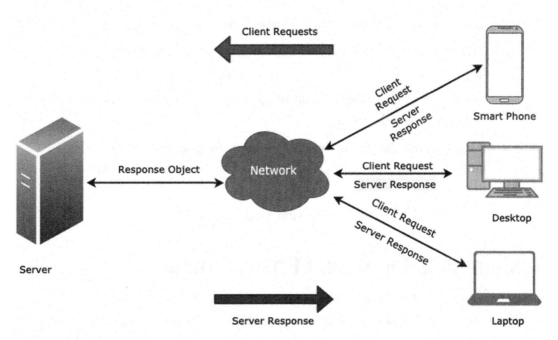

Figure 8-4. *Client-server architectural model*

In the diagram in Figure 8-4, various clients send requests to a server to access data. The server replies with appropriate responses. This is based on standard protocols.

Advantages of the Client-Server Model

The following are some of the advantages of the client-server model.

- It is a centralized system. All the data is stored in one place (i.e., on the server-side).

- It is easy to maintain, upgrade, and integrate new services.

- Clients and servers may be located in any place in the world; they can access data.

- Data is secure because only authorized people have access to confidential data.

- Data recovery is possible with an advanced storage mechanism on the server side.

Disadvantages of the Client-Server Model

The following are some of the disadvantages of the client-server model.

- If there is an issue on the server-side, then the client does not get any response from the server.

- Servers are prone to DoS (denial-of-service) and DDoS (distributed denial-of-service) attacks.

- It is not a cost-effective approach because setting up a server requires more space geographically, and maintenance requires manpower that ultimately increases the cost.

- Several kinds of attacks are possible on this architecture.

System Calls for Socket Programming

IPC over a network is done with socket programming. The necessary system calls to develop programs make use of sockets. The<sys/socket.h> library contains all the system calls for socket programming. The most commonly used system calls are socket(), bind(), listen(), accept(), send(), receive(), write(), read(), sendto(), recvfrom(), and close().

socket()

A socket() system call creates an endpoint for the communication of certain socket types. This system call creates a socket that returns a socket file descriptor on successful creation. If any error occurs, it returns –1. The socket() system call creates a simple interface for communication, but it doesn't have any information about the sender and receiver.

The following shows the syntax.

`int socket(int domain, int type, int protocol)`

`domain` deals with the type of communication domain for establishing communication. It describes the protocol family. The most common protocol families are AF_INET(IP v.4 Protocol) and AF_INET6 (IP v.6 Protocol).

The **type** argument describes the data transfer format between two communicating systems. Certain semantics are available to use a format to send and receive the data. The semantics that commonly are commonly used are described in Table 8-1.

Table 8-1. *Semantics*

Semantic	Description
SOCK_ STREAM	It provides connection-oriented, stable, and reliable communication between two systems.
SOCK_ DGRAM	It provides connectionless communication between two systems. Communication is unreliable and data should be in fixed length.
SOCK_RAW	It establishes the communication system based on a raw network protocol.
SOCK_RDM	It provides a reliable datagram layer for communication that doesn't guarantee the order of messages transferred to the receiver.

- **protocol** takes the protocol value that is used for communication purposes. The value for an Internet Protocol is 0 by default.

bind()

A bind() system call binds the socket with a port number and address. The return type of this system call is an integer. It returns 0 if a success and –1 if any failure occurs.

The following shows the syntax.

```
int bind(int sockfd,
         const struct sockaddr *addr,
         socklen_t addrlen)
```

- **sockfd** takes the coket descriptor that is created using the socket() system call.

- **addr** describes the address structure for the socket that binds with the created socket interface/descriptor. The structure of the socket address structure is as follows.

```
struct sockaddr {
    sa_family_t sa_family; // Address Family
    char sa_data[14];      // Family Specific Address Info
}
```

- **size** takes the size (in bytes) for the socket address structure.

listen()

A listen() system call listens for the connections on a socket. It is a nonblocking system call that waits continuously to make a connection with the client. This system call waits for the client to establish a connection. The socket is in passive mode until the client connects to it. The return type of this system call is an integer. It returns 0 if it is listening properly and returns –1 if any error occurs.

The following shows the syntax.

```
int listen(int sockfd, int backlog)
```

- sockfd takes the socket file descriptor as an argument created using the socket() system call.

- backlog takes the parameter of the maximum length of the queue.
  This length determines the number of connections that are possible
  with that socket. Once the limit is reached and any new socket
  connection is trying to establish a connection, the connecting socket
  gets an error.

accept()

An accept() system call is used only for connection-based socket types. It takes the first
connection request from the queue and creates a new file descriptor referring to the
request socket. The return type of this system call is an integer. It returns a file descriptor
value for the accepted socket if a success and returns –1 if any failure occurs.

The following shows the syntax.

```
int accept(int sockfd,
        struct sockaddr *addr,
        socklen_t *addrlen)
```

- sockaddr takes the socket descriptor that is created using the socket()
  system call.

- addr takes the socket address structure of the peer socket to establish
  a connection. It is the client address of the connected socket.

- addrlen takes the length of the peer address (i.e., client address)
  length.

send()

A send() system call sends data to another socket. This system call only works when
the socket is in a connected state; otherwise, it throws an error. The return type of this
system call is ssize_t. It returns the number of bytes sent to the peer if a success and
returns –1 if any failure occurs.

The following shows the syntax.

```
ssize_t send(int sockfd,
        const void *buf,
        size_t len,
        int flags)
```

- sockfd takes the socket descriptor that is created using the socket system call.

- The buf (buffer) parameter takes the message object that you want to transmit to the peer connection.

- len takes the length of the message (in bytes) to transmit to a peer connection.

- flags are external flags that handle certain exceptions while transmitting data. Usually, you set this value to 0.

recv()

A recv() system call receives the message/data from a peer/connected socket. The return type of this system is ssize_t. It returns the length of the message (in bytes) that are received from the socket. It returns –1 if any failure occurs.

The following shows the syntax.

```
ssize_t recv(int sockfd,
             void *buf,
             size_t len,
             int flags)
```

- **sockfd** is the socket descriptor created using the socket() system call.

- **buf** is a message that is received from the connected socket.

- **len** is the length of the message/data that is being received.

- **flags** takes the external flags to handle the exceptions.

Note   send() and recv() system calls only work for the connection-oriented protocols (i.e., TCP). When you want to work with the UDP protocol, you need to use the sendto() and recvfrom() system calls to send and receive the data.

---

sendto()

A sendto() system call sends data to the connected socket. It returns the number of bytes that are being sent to the socket. It returns –1 if any failure occurs.

The following shows the syntax.

```
ssize_t sendto(int sockfd,
               const void *buf,
               size_t len,
               int flags,
               const struct sockaddr *dest_addr,
               socklen_t addrlen)
```

- **sockfd** is a socket descriptor that is created using a socket() system call.

- **buf** is message/data that is sent to the socket.

- **len** is the length of the data in bytes that is sent to the socket address.

- **flags** handles exceptions while transmitting the data.

- **destaddr** takes the address of the destination socket.

- addrlen takes the address length of the destination address.

recvfrom()

A recvfrom() system call receives the message/data from the socket. It returns the number of bytes received from the socket. It returns –1 if any failures occur.

The following shows the syntax.

```
ssize_t recvfrom(int sockfd,
                 void *buf,
                 size_t len,
                 int flags,
                 struct sockaddr *src_addr,
                 socklen_t *addrlen)
```

- **sockfd** takes the socket descriptor using the socket() system call.

- buf is the message/data to send to the socket.

- len is the message length being transmitted.

- **flags** handles exceptions while transmitting data.

- srcaddr takes the address of the client.

- addrlen takes the length of the client address.

Note   write() and read() system calls also send and receive data.

---

close()

A close() system call closes the connection once usage is completed. It also frees up the port that is used by the socket. It returns 0 if a success and –1 if any failure occurs.

The following shows the syntax.

int close(int sockfd)

sockfd takes the socket descriptor that you want to close.

Implementation of Client Server Architecture

This section discusses the implementation of client-server architecture using the TCP and UDP protocols. TCP guarantees data delivery to the client, whereas UDP does not guarantee data delivery. The mechanisms of data transfer differ from TCP to UDP. This section discusses the TCP and UDP mechanisms and uses practical examples.

TCP Client-Server Architecture

TCP is a connection-oriented protocol. There are certain steps to follow to build your own TCP network connection. This connection is built with the socket API. A client-server architecture has clients and servers.

In a single client-server architecture, you build a single client and server on your machine to communicate with each other. The advantage of using a TCP connection for developing a socket connection is that it guarantees data delivery. It also maintains the order of the data that is being transmitted. This connection is reliable and uses the three-way handshake principle for data transfer. SOCK_STREM is used while creating the socket. The entire process can be divided into two major parts: the server and the client.

The task of the server is to provide services to a client based on his request.

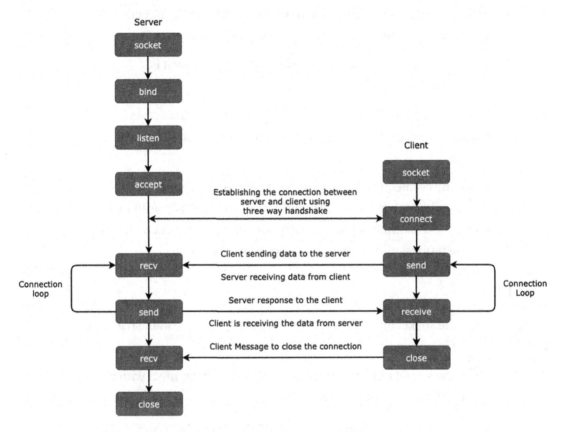

Figure 8-5. *TCP Client-server implementation architecture*

TCP Server

Using the socket function, a socket will create on the system, which acts as a bidirectional device.

1. The connection takes the IP address and the port number to bind together, making the socket ready for use.

2. The socket listens to the client's request by making the socket connection open. Once the request hits the server, it accepts the invitation from the client.

3. The accepted invitation establishes the client-server connection. The data delivery in TCP is done with three-way handshaking, in which there is an acknowledgment between the client and server after data is transferred.

4. When a client sends a request to the server after the connection is reestablished, the server takes the request and processes it.

5. The server sends the data to the client after the request is processed.

6. When a client sends the close connection request, the server closes the connection between the client device and the server device.

7. Once the connection is established, a connection loop communicates with the server and client continuously until the client makes a closing request to the server. Once the client sends a close request, the connection is closed by the server.

TCP Client

The client uses the socket function to create a socket object to establish a connection with a remote or local server.

1. Once the socket object is being created, it tries to connect with a server IP address and port number.

2. Once a connection is established, the client sends the request to the server for processing.

3. The server processes the request and responds to the client. Then the client, accepts/receives the response that is being sent by the server.

4. When the client sends the close request to the server, the server closes the request that is created between the client and the server.

TCP Client-Server Code

Now let's look at the implementation of the client and server separately in C. First, let's build the server code to provide services to the client using socket programming. After that, let's build the client code using the same socket programming.

Server Code

Here is the server code.

```
#include<stdio.h>
#include<stdlib.h>
#include<unistd.h>
#include<string.h>
#include<sys/socket.h>
#include<sys/types.h>
#include<netdb.h>
#include<netinet/in.h>

#define MESSAGE_LENGTH 1024 // Maximum number of data that can transfer
#define PORT 8888 // port number to connect
#define SA struct sockaddr // Creating Macro for the socketaddr as SA

struct sockaddr_in serveraddress, client;
socklen_t length;
Int sockert_file_descriptor, connection, bind_status, connection_status;
char message[MESSAGE_LENGTH];

int main(){

    // Creating the Socket
    sockert_file_descriptor = socket(AF_INET, SOCK_STREAM, 0);

    if(sockert_file_descriptor == -1){
        printf("Scoket creation failed.!\n");
        exit(1);
    }
```

```
// Erases the memory
bzero(&serveraddress, sizeof(serveraddress));

// Server Properties
serveraddress.sin_addr.s_addr = htonl(INADDR_ANY);
// Setting the port number
serveraddress.sin_port = htons(PORT);
// Protocol family
serveraddress.sin_family = AF_INET;

// Binding the newly created socket with the given Ip Address
bind_status = bind(sockert_file_descriptor, (SA*)&serveraddress,
sizeof(serveraddress));

if(bind_status == -1){
    printf("Socket binding failed.!\n");
    exit(1);
}

// Server is listening for new creation
connection_status = listen(sockert_file_descriptor, 5);

if(connection_status == -1){
    printf("Socket is unable to listen for new connections.!\n");
    exit(1);
}else{
    printf("Server is listening for new connection: \n");
}

length =  sizeof(client);

connection = accept(sockert_file_descriptor, (SA*)&client, &length);

if(connection == -1){
    printf("Server is unable to accept the data from client.!\n");
    exit(1);
}

// Communication Establishment
    while(1){
```

```
    bzero(message, MESSAGE_LENGTH);

    read(connection, message, sizeof(message));

    if (strncmp("end", message, 3) == 0) {
        printf("Client Exited.\n");
        printf("Server is Exiting..!\n");
        break;
    }

    printf("Data received from client: %s\n", message);
    bzero(message, MESSAGE_LENGTH);

    printf("Enter the message you want to send to the client: ");
    scanf("%[^\n]%*c", message);

     // Sending the data to the server by storing the number of bytes
        transferred in bytes variable
    ssize_t bytes = write(connection, message, sizeof(message));

    // If the number of bytes is >= 0 then the data is sent successfully
    if(bytes >= 0){
        printf("Data successfully sent to the client.!\n");
    }

}
// Closing the Socket Connection
close(sockert_file_descriptor);

return 0;
}
```

This code is responsible for the entire server functionality. Initially, the socket function creates the socket object. If the socket is unable to be created, the program immediately throws an error. Once the socket is created, the bzero() function erases the data of the object being created. The data might be in a string format.

After the socket object is created, it binds the client IP address and port number. The server sets the type of Internet family and the data transfer mode. In any case, if binding the IP and port fails, it throws an error.

Now the server is listening to establish a connection. If the server is unable to listen, the server exits the connection loop. If the client sends the data, the server accepts the data. If any error occurs, the server exists. An infinite while loop receives data from the client and sends the appropriate response to the client. If the client sends the message as 'end', both the client and server are terminated. You can customize the code for your own purposes.

Client Code

Here is the client code.

```
#include<stdio.h>
#include<stdlib.h>
#include<unistd.h>
#include<string.h>
#include<sys/socket.h>
#include<netdb.h>
#include<arpa/inet.h>

// Maximum number of data that can transfer
#define MESSAGE_LENGTH 1024
#define PORT 8888 // port number to connect
// Creating Macro for the socketaddr as SA
#define SA struct sockaddr
// Global Data
int socket_file_descriptor, connection;
struct sockaddr_in serveraddress, client;
char message[MESSAGE_LENGTH];

int main(){

    // Socket Creation
    socket_file_descriptor = socket(AF_INET, SOCK_STREAM, 0);
    if(socket_file_descriptor == -1){
        printf("Creation of Socket failed.!\n");
        exit(1);
    }
```

```c
// Erases the memory
bzero(&serveraddress, sizeof(serveraddress));

// Setting the Server Properties
serveraddress.sin_addr.s_addr = inet_addr("127.0.0.1");
// Setting the port number
serveraddress.sin_port = htons(PORT);
// Protocol family
serveraddress.sin_family = AF_INET;

// Establishing the Connection with server
connection = connect(socket_file_descriptor, (SA*)&serveraddress,
sizeof(serveraddress));

if(connection == -1){
    printf("Connection with the server failed.!\n");
    exit(1);
}

// Interacting with the server

while(1){

    bzero(message, sizeof(message));

    printf("Enter the message you want to send to the server: ");
    scanf("%[^\n]%*c", message);

     if ((strncmp(message, "end", 3)) == 0) {
        write(socket_file_descriptor, message, sizeof(message));
        printf("Client Exit.\n");
        break;
    }

    // Sending the data to the server by storing the number of bytes
        transferred in bytes variable
    ssize_t bytes = write(socket_file_descriptor, message, sizeof(message));
```

```
    // If the number of bytes is >= 0 then the data is sent successfully
    if(bytes >= 0){
        printf("Data send to the server successfully.!\n");
    }

    bzero(message, sizeof(message));

    // Reading the response from the server.
    read(socket_file_descriptor, message, sizeof(message));

    printf("Data received from server: %s\n", message);

}
// Closing the Socket Connection
close(socket_file_descriptor);

return 0;
}
```

This code is for the client who initially creates the socket using the socket function. It binds the server IP address and port number by using the bind function. The client connects to the server using the connect() function. If the connection is successful, the client can send the message; otherwise, it throws an error. An infinite loop sends the request to the server using the write() system call. It receives the response from the server through the read() system call. If the client sends the close request, as shown in Figure 8-5, the server closes the connection.

Here is the output.

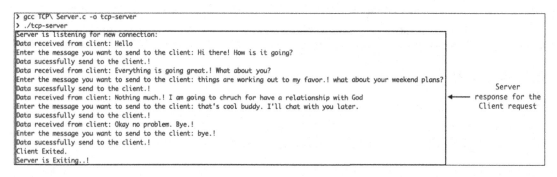

Figure 8-6. Output of TCP server

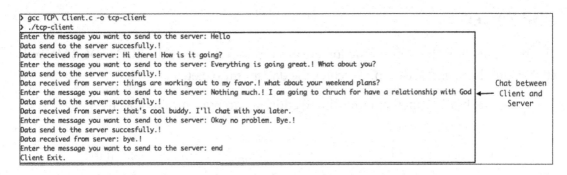

```
> gcc TCP\ Client.c -o tcp-client
> ./tcp-client
Enter the message you want to send to the server: Hello
Data send to the server succesfully.!
Data received from server: Hi there! How is it going?
Enter the message you want to send to the server: Everything is going great.! What about you?
Data send to the server succesfully.!
Data received from server: things are working out to my favor.! what about your weekend plans?
Enter the message you want to send to the server: Nothing much.! I am going to chruch for have a relationship with God
Data send to the server succesfully.!
Data received from server: that's cool buddy. I'll chat with you later.
Enter the message you want to send to the server: Okay no problem. Bye.!
Data send to the server succesfully.!
Data received from server: bye.!
Enter the message you want to send to the server: end
Client Exit.
```

Chat between Client and Server

Figure 8-7. *Output of the client connected to TCP server*

UDP Client Server Architecture

UDP is different from a TCP connection. It is a connectionless protocol, whereas TCP is a connection-oriented protocol. In this architecture data, packets do not guarantee delivery to the client. It is not a reliable protocol. Unlike TCP, it doesn't connect with the server; instead, the connection client sends the datagram packets to the server. When the server receives datagram packets from the client, it accepts the them. A datagram packet contains the address of the sender, which helps the server send it to the client. The working mechanism of the UDP client-server architecture are represented in Figure 8-8.

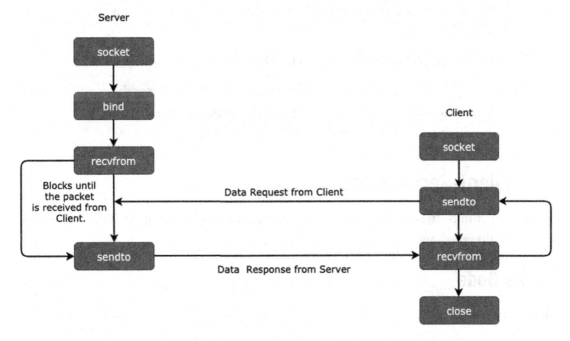

Figure 8-8. *UDP client-server implementation architecture*

UDP Server

On the server-side, the socket function creates the socket. It uses the SOCK_DGRAM and IF_NET for the socket creation. It creates the datagram socket.

- The bind() function binds the IP address and port number together for the connection.

- The recvfrom() function waits for the datagram from the client. If the datagram arrives, it accepts the data and works on it.

- The sendto() function sends the processed data to the client using the client address present in the datagram header.

UDP Client

On the client-side, the same socket function creates the socket, and it uses the SOCK_DGRAM to create the UDP-based client system.

- After the socket is created, there is no connection required, like TCP. In this architecture, a datagram is sent to the server using the address of the server.

- The sendto() function sends datagram packets to the server as a request.

- The recvfrom() function receives the data from the server.

- The close() function closes the connection. The client closes the connection once the packet is received. If the packet is not received, the client waits. This is the drawback of the UDP protocol.

UDP Client-Server Code

This section builds the client-server architecture using the UDP protocol. First, let's build server architecture, and then build the client architecture.

Server Code

Here is the server code.

```c
#include <stdio.h>
#include<stdlib.h>
#include<unistd.h>
#include <strings.h>
#include <sys/types.h>
#include <arpa/inet.h>
#include <sys/socket.h>
#include<netinet/in.h>
// Maximum number of bytes that can transfer and receive.
#define MESSAGE_BUFFER 4096
#define PORT 8888 // port number to connect
// Creating Macro for the socketaddr as SA
#define SA struct sockaddr

// Global Data
char buffer[MESSAGE_BUFFER];
char message[MESSAGE_BUFFER];
int socket_file_descriptor, message_size;
socklen_t length;
const char *end_string = "end";
int quit_status;
struct sockaddr_in serveraddress, client;

void processRequest(){

    // Server Properties
    bzero(&serveraddress, sizeof(serveraddress));
    // Create a UDP Socket via PORT 8888
    socket_file_descriptor = socket(AF_INET, SOCK_DGRAM, 0);
    serveraddress.sin_addr.s_addr = htonl(INADDR_ANY);
    // Connecting via port 8888
    serveraddress.sin_port = htons(PORT);
    // Protocol Family
    serveraddress.sin_family = AF_INET;
    // bind server address to socket descriptor
    bind(socket_file_descriptor, (SA*)&serveraddress, sizeof(serveraddress));
```

```c
    while(1){
        // Calculating the Client Datagram length
        length = sizeof(client);
        message_size = recvfrom(socket_file_descriptor, buffer,
        sizeof(buffer), 0, (SA*)&client,&length);

        buffer[message_size] = '\0';
        quit_status = strcmp(buffer, end_string);

        if(quit_status == 0){
            printf("Server is Quitting\n");
            close(socket_file_descriptor);
            exit(0);
        }
        printf("Message Received from Client: %s\n",buffer);
        // sending the response to the client
        printf("Enter reply message to the client: ");
        scanf("%[^\n]%*c", message);
        sendto(socket_file_descriptor, message, MESSAGE_BUFFER, 0,
        (SA*)&client, sizeof(client));
        printf("Message Sent Successfully to the client: %s\n", message);
        printf("Waiting for the Reply from Client..!\n");
    }
    // Closing the Socket File Descriptor.
    close(socket_file_descriptor);
}
int main() {

    printf("SERVER IS LISTENING THROUGH THE PORT: %d WITHIN A LOCAL
    SYSTEM\n", PORT);
    // Calling the process request function to process the client request
        and give the response.
    processRequest();
    return 0;
}
```

In this code, the socket function creates the socket and binds the IP address and the port number. The recvfrom function receives the datagram from the client, and the sendto function sends the data packet to the client. The processRequest function does all the activities of the server, like receiving the data, processing the data, and sending the data/response to the client. The output of the server architecture is shown in Figure 8-9.

Client Code

Finally, the client.

```
#include<stdio.h>
#include<unistd.h>
#include<stdlib.h>
#include<strings.h>
#include<sys/socket.h> // To work with socket programming
#include<sys/types.h>
#include<arpa/inet.h>
#include<netinet/in.h>
// Maximum number of bytes that can transfer and receive.
#define MESSAGE_BUFFER 4096
#define PORT 8888 // port number to connect
// Creating Macro for the socketaddr as SA
#define SA struct sockaddr

// Global Data
char buffer[MESSAGE_BUFFER];
char message[MESSAGE_BUFFER];

int socket_file_descriptor, n;
int size = 0;
int quit_status;
const char *end_string = "end";
struct sockaddr_in serveraddress;

void sendRequest(){

    // Setting the properties to connect with Server
    bzero(&serveraddress, sizeof(serveraddress));
```

```
// Working with Localhost Address
serveraddress.sin_addr.s_addr = inet_addr("127.0.0.1");
// Connecting via port 8888
serveraddress.sin_port = htons(PORT);
// Protocol Family
serveraddress.sin_family = AF_INET;
// creating the datagram socket
socket_file_descriptor = socket(AF_INET, SOCK_DGRAM, 0);

// Establishing a connection with the server.
if(connect(socket_file_descriptor, (SA *)&serveraddress,
sizeof(serveraddress)) < 0) {
    printf("\n Something went wrong Connection Failed \n");
    exit(1);
}

while(1){

printf("Enter a message you want to send to the server: ");
scanf("%[^\n]%*c", message);
quit_status = strcmp(message, end_string);

if(quit_status == 0){
    sendto(socket_file_descriptor, message, MESSAGE_BUFFER, 0, (SA*)
    NULL, sizeof(serveraddress));
    printf("Client work is done.!\n");
    close(socket_file_descriptor);
    exit(0);
}else{
    sendto(socket_file_descriptor, message, MESSAGE_BUFFER, 0, (SA*)
    NULL, sizeof(serveraddress));
    printf("Message sent successfully to the server: %s\n", message);
    printf("Waiting for the Response from Server..!\n");
}
```

```
        printf("Message Received From Server: ");
        recvfrom(socket_file_descriptor, buffer, sizeof(buffer), 0, (SA*)
        NULL, NULL);
        printf("%s\n", buffer);
    }
    // closing the Socket File Descriptor
    close(socket_file_descriptor);
}

int main() {

    printf("CLIENT IS ESTABLISHING A CONNECTION WITH SERVER THROUGH PORT:
    %d\n", PORT);
    // Calling the Send Request to send a request to the server.
    sendRequest();
    return 0;
}
```

In the client code, the socket function creates the socket and binds the IP address and the port number. The sendto function sends the request to the server (i.e., datagram packets). The recvfrom function receives a datagram from the server. The close function closes the connection. The sendRequest function connects with the remote/local server, sends the data/request to the server, and accepts the response from the server if the server sends any response.

Figure 8-9 is the output.

```
> gcc UDP\ Server.c -o udp-server
> ./udp-server
SERVER IS LISTENING THROUGH THE PORT: 8888 WITHIN A LOCAL SYSTEM
Message Received from Client: Hello Buddy.!
Enter reply message to the client: Hello.! How is it going?
Message Sent Succesfully to the client: Hello.! How is it going?
Waiting for the Reply from Client..!
Message Received from Client: It's going great.! How about you?        Server is responding
Enter reply message to the client: Everything is cool.          ◄——— to the Client Requests.
Message Sent Succesfully to the client: Everything is cool.
Waiting for the Reply from Client..!
Message Received from Client: Okay then Bye.!
Enter reply message to the client: Bye.!
Message Sent Succesfully to the client: Bye.!
Waiting for the Reply from Client..!
Server is Quitting
```

Figure 8-9. *UDP server output*

265

The workings of the client application are shown in Figure 8-10.

```
> gcc UDP\ Client.c -o udp-client
> ./udp-client
CLIENT IS ESTABLISHING A CONNECTION WITH SERVER THROUGH PORT: 8888
Enter a message you want to send to the server: Hello Buddy.!
Message sent successfully to the server: Hello Buddy.!
Waiting for the Response from Server..!
Message Received From Server: Hello.! How is it going?
Enter a message you want to send to the server: It's going great.! How about you?      Real time communication between
Message sent successfully to the server: It's going great.! How about you?         ←──── Client and Server
Waiting for the Response from Server..!                                                 using UDP Protocol.
Message Received From Server: Everything is cool.
Enter a message you want to send to the server: Okay then Bye.!
Message sent successfully to the server: Okay then Bye.!
Waiting for the Response from Server..!
Message Received From Server: Bye.!
Enter a message you want to send to the server: end
Client work is done.!
```

Figure 8-10. *Output of the client connected to UDP server*

Summary

This chapter discussed socket programming with C and how to achieve IPC over a
network. The chapter covered various topics, like the OSI architectural model and the
TCP/IP model. You saw implementations of client-server architecture using TCP and
UDP protocols as well. You also completed various IPC techniques between processes.

Index

© Sri Manikanta Palakollu 2021
S. M. Palakollu, *Practical System Programming with C*, https://doi.org/10.1007/978-1-4842-6321-1

Printed in the United States
By Bookmasters